The Azar Grammar Series

TEST BANK for
BASIC
ENGLISH
GRAMMAR

Second Edition

Helene Rubinstein Pitzer

Mark Wade Lieu

Test Coordinator

Publisher: *Mary Jane Peluso*
Development Editor: *Andrea Bryant*
Editorial Supervisor: *Janet Johnston*
Director of Production and Manufacturing: *Aliza Greenblatt*
Executive Managing Editor: *Dominick Mosco*
Electronic Production Editor: *Michelle LoGerfo*
Art Director: *Merle Krumper*
Cover Designer: *Joel Mitnick Design*
Manufacturing Manager: *Ray Keating*

Illustrator: *Michelle LoGerfo*

Printed in the United States of America

10 9 8 7 6 5 4 3

ISBN 0-13-788480-X

Contents

Introduction vi

CHAPTER 1 USING BE AND HAVE

Quiz 1 Singular and plural nouns; A and AN; BE verbs 1
Quiz 2 BE verbs, negatives with BE verbs, adjectives with BE verbs 2
Quiz 3 BE + prepositions of location 3
Quiz 4 WHERE + BE questions; YES/NO questions with BE 4
Quiz 5 BE verbs; HAS and HAVE 4
Quiz 6 Using THIS and THAT, THESE and THOSE 4
Quiz 7 WHAT and WHO 5
Chapter 1 Test 6

CHAPTER 2 EXPRESSING PRESENT TIME (PART 1)

Quiz 1 The simple present tense + frequency adverbs 9
Quiz 2 HAVE/HAS; DO/DOES; GO/GOES 10
Quiz 3 YES/NO questions using DO/DOES and negatives 11
Quiz 4 Information questions 12
Quiz 5 Dictation 12
Quiz 6 IT (time) 13
Quiz 7 IT (weather) 14
Chapter 2 Test 15

CHAPTER 3 EXPRESSING PRESENT TIME (PART 2)

Quiz 1 The present progressive 17
Quiz 2 Using the present progressive 18
Quiz 3 Simple present vs. present progressive 18
Quiz 4 Nonaction verbs 19
Quiz 5 NEED and WANT, WOULD LIKE, THINK ABOUT, and THINK THAT 20
Quiz 6 THERE + BE statements and questions 21
Quiz 7 Prepositions of location 22
Chapter 3 Test 23

CHAPTER 4 NOUNS AND PRONOUNS

Quiz 1   Subjects and objects; adjective + noun 26
Quiz 2   Subject and object pronouns 27
Quiz 3   Plural nouns 27
Quiz 4   Irregular plurals 28
Quiz 5   Count and noncount 29
Quiz 6   A/AN and SOME; units of measure 30
Quiz 7   THE and Ø 31
Quiz 8   Indefinite pronouns 31
Chapter 4 Test **32**

CHAPTER 5 EXPRESSING PAST TIME

Quiz 1   Past tense of BE, questions, negatives 34
Quiz 2   Simple past tense; past time words 34
Quiz 3   Irregular past tense verbs 35
Quiz 4   Irregular past tense verbs; questions and negatives 35
Quiz 5   WH-questions 36
Quiz 6   WHAT and WHO questions 36
Quiz 7   Time clauses with BEFORE, AFTER, and WHEN 37
Chapter 5 Test **38**

MIDTERM EXAM **41**

CHAPTER 6 EXPESSING FUTURE TIME

Quiz 1   BE GOING TO 47
Quiz 2   Future and past time words 48
Quiz 3   WILL 49
Quiz 4   Future tense questions 50
Quiz 5   MAY, MIGHT, and MAYBE 50
Quiz 6   Future time clauses with BEFORE, AFTER, and WHEN 51
Quiz 7   IF-clauses in future and habitual present 51
Chapter 6 Test **52**

CHAPTER 7 EXPRESSING ABILITY

Quiz 1   CAN, KNOW HOW TO, and COULD 55
Quiz 2   VERY, TOO, TOO MUCH, and TOO MANY 56
Quiz 3   TOO + adjective, adjective + ENOUGH, and ENOUGH 56
Quiz 4   BE ABLE TO; polite questions 58
Quiz 5   Imperatives 58
Quiz 6   AT and IN for location 59
Chapter 7 Test **60**

CHAPTER 8 NOUNS, PRONOUNS, AND ADJECTIVES

Quiz 1   Noun and adjective modifiers; word order of adjectives 62
Quiz 2   Expressions of quantity; subject-verb agreement 63
Quiz 3   Possessive nouns and pronouns; WHOSE questions 63
Quiz 4   Noun + conjunction + noun 64
Quiz 5   Indirect objects with TO and FOR 64
Quiz 6   Indirect objects with BUY, GET, and MAKE 65
Chapter 8 Test **66**

CHAPTER 9 MAKING COMPARISONS

Quiz 1   HE SAME, SIMILAR, DIFFERENT, LIKE, and ALIKE 69
Quiz 2   -ER and MORE 70
Quiz 3   AS . . .AS; LESS THAN 70
Quiz 4   Using BUT 71
Quiz 5   ONE OF + superlative 71
Quiz 6   Adjectives and adverbs 72
Quiz 7   Comparisons with adverbs 73
Chapter 9 Test **74**

CHAPTER 10 EXPRESSING IDEAS WITH VERBS

Quiz 1   SHOULD and LET'S 76
Quiz 2   MUST and HAVE TO 77
Quiz 3   Review of modals 78
Quiz 4   Present and past progressive 78
Quiz 5   WHILE, WHEN, and simple past versus past progressive 79
Quiz 6   FOR and SINCE. 80
Quiz 7   Present perfect questions and NEVER/EVER 81
Quiz 8   Irregular past participles and HOW LONG questions 82
Chapter 10 Test **83**

FINAL EXAM **85**

ANSWER KEY **89**

Introduction

This Test Bank was developed to accompany *Basic English Grammar, Second Edition*. For each chapter, there are short quizzes of 5 to 15 items for a related group of grammatical points. The quizzes are designed to be completed in approximately ten minutes, permitting the teacher to use the quizzes to do quick checks of student understanding and to use what has been taught. Each chapter ends with a comprehensive chapter test. The formats of the questions in the chapter tests follow those used in previous quizzes. In this way, students are prepared for the format of the chapter test as well as for its content. Also included are a midterm exam and a final exam that can be used in conjunction with the other tests and quizzes or separately.

The quizzes, tests, and exams are already formatted for easy duplication. Each set of items is accompanied by specific directions. Permission is granted to duplicate as many copies as needed for the classroom use only.

Great care has been taken to provide valid and appropriate items in all tests and quizzes. Students will encounter a wide variety of test formats, from closed formats such as multiple choice and matching, to more open formats such as sentence writing and completion and error identification. The answer key provides definitive answers where possible and examples of acceptable answers where a variety of responses is possible.

CHAPTER 1
Using *Be* and *Have*

■ **Quiz 1:** Singular and plural nouns; A and AN; BE verbs.

Complete the sentences. Use *is* or *are* and a singular or plural form of the nouns in the list.

bird	flower	month
city	insect	✔ season
continent	language	
country	machine	

Example: Summer _____*is a season*_____.

1. Japanese _____.

   Japan _____.

2. Spain and France _____.

   Spanish and French _____.

3. Los Angeles _____.

   Paris and Rome _____.

4. Ants _____.

   A butterfly _____.

5. March _____.

   October and November _____.

6. Winter and spring _____.

   Fall _____.

7. North America _____.

   Europe and Africa _____.

8. A lily _____.

   Roses _____.

9. Typewriters _____.

   A computer _____.

10. A chicken _____.

    Ducks _____.

■ **Quiz 2:** BE verbs, negatives with BE verbs, adjectives with BE verbs.

Write sentences to describe the pictures. Use *is*, *isn't*, *are*, or *aren't* and an adjective from the list. Use each adjective only once.

angry	happy	soft
beautiful	✔ healthy	square
expensive	new	young
fast	open	

Example: Sam ___*isn't*___ sick. He ___*is healthy*___ .

1. Bob _____ old. He _____.

   He _____ sad. He _____.

   A motorcycle _____ slow.

   It _____ .

2. The table _____ round.

   It _____ .

   The flowers _____ ugly.

   They _____ .

   The windows _____ closed.

   They _____ .

   The chairs _____ hard.

   They _____ .

3. The blouse _____ old.

   It _____ .

   It _____ cheap.

   It _____ .

   The woman _____ happy.

   She _____ .

■ **Quiz 3:**   BE + prepositions of location.

Complete the sentences with prepositions from the list. You may use a preposition more than once.

above	at	behind	in	on	next to

Example: Mike and Ann are _____*at*_____ home.

1. Ann is _____ her room.

2. She is _____ her desk.

3. Ann's computer is _____ her desk.

4. Her cat is _____ her.

5. Mike is _____ his bed.

6. His lamp is _____ his bed.

7. His newspaper is _____ his hands.

8. His books are _____ a shelf.

9. The shelf is _____ his bed.

■ **Quiz 4:** WHERE + BE questions; YES/NO questions with BE.

Match the questions and answers and write the letter in the blank.

<u>d</u> 1. Is Ms. Black an artist?   a. It's on the east coast of the United States.

_____ 2. Where are Yoko and Rita?   b. Yes, I am.

_____ 3. Where is New York?   c. No, I don't. I live in Los Angeles.

_____ 4. Is this exercise a quiz?   d. No, she's not. She's a bus driver.

_____ 5. Are you happy?   e. No, it isn't. It's an insect.

_____ 6. Do you live in Miami?   f. Yes, it is.

_____ 7. Is a fly a bird?   g. It's at the corner of Smith and Charles Streets.

_____ 8. Where is the bus stop?   h. No, they're not.

_____ 9. Where is your pen?   i. It's in my hand.

_____ 10. Are John and Sue married?   j. They're at the library.

■ **Quiz 5:** BE verbs; HAS and HAVE.

Write a paragraph of four or more sentences about a classmate. Tell about the person's profession, appearance, and nationality. Use the verbs **be** and **have**.

_____ is a student in my English class. _____

_____

_____

_____

_____

_____

■ **Quiz 6:** Using THIS and THAT, THESE and THOSE.

Your teacher will point to items in the classroom and will dictate sentences to the class. Write down the sentences.

Examples: This is my desk.   That's his book.
                These are my books.   Those are her shoes.

_____

_____

_____

_____

■ **Quiz 7:** WHAT and WHO.

Each **B** sentence answers a question. Write a *who* or *what* question for each answer.

Example: **A:** _____ *What is a chicken?* _____

B: A bird. (A chicken is a bird.)

1. **A:** _____
   B: A small animal. (A cat is a small animal.)

2. **A:** _____
   B: My neighbors. (Those people are my neighbors.)

3. **A:** _____
   B: My teacher. (That's my teacher.)

4. **A:** _____
   B: English. (My favorite class is English.)

5. **A:** _____
   B: Ali and Susan. (Their names are Ali and Susan.)

6. **A:** _____
   B: Peter. (His name is Peter.)

7. **A:** _____
   B: 555-5000. (Her telephone number is 555-5000.)

8. **A:** _____
   B: Ms. Black. (Her teacher is Ms. Black.)

9. **A:** _____
   B: A large animal. (A camel is a large animal.)

10. **A:** _____
    B: A car. (A Cadillac is a car.)

■ CHAPTER 1 TEST

A. Write a paragraph of at least ten sentences about Yoko, Alex, and Pablo, who are students in Ms. Rice's ESL class.

	Yoko	**Alex**	**Pablo**
Male or Female?	Female	Male	Male
City	Tokyo	Frankfurt	Mexico City
Home Country	Japan	Germany	Mexico
Married or Single?	Married	Single	Married
Description	Black hair, brown eyes, 25 years old, friendly	Brown hair, blue eyes, short, 32 years old, serious	Brown hair, green eyes, 28 years old, shy

Yoko, Alex, and Pablo are students in Ms. Rice's ESL class. _____

_____

_____

_____

_____

_____

_____

_____

_____

_____

_____

_____

_____

_____

_____

_____

B. Write a question for each answer, using the cues in parentheses.

    Example: **A:** _____*Are you at work now?*_____

               B: Yes, I am. (I am at work now.)

1. **A:** _____
   B: Yes, she is. (Marta is my wife.)

2. **A:** _____
   B: Yes, they are. (These are my classmates.)

3. **A:** _____
   B: No, she isn't. (Sonia isn't tall.)

4. **A:** _____
   B: No, I'm not. (I'm not at home right now.)

5. **A:** _____
   B: No, he's not. (Sam isn't tired.)

6. **A:** _____
   B: They're cities. (Montreal and Miami are cities.)

7. **A:** _____
   B: Kate. (Her name is Kate.)

8. **A:** _____
   B: Yes, she is. (Kate is married.)

9. **A:** _____
   B: A test. (This is a test.)

10. **A:** _____
    B: Ms. Rice. (My favorite teacher is Ms. Rice.)

C. Complete the sentences with prepositions from the list. You may use a preposition more than once.

beside	between	in	next to	on

The book is _____ the clown's head.

The vase is _____ the book.

The flowers are _____ the vase.

The vase is _____ the two boxes.

The ball is _____ the clown's foot.

The dog is _____ the clown.

D. Add prepositions to complete the sentences that describe the picture.

The milk is _____ the top shelf.

The eggs are _____ the cheese.

The carrots are _____ the eggs.

The woman is _____ the door.

CHAPTER 2
Expressing Present Time (Part 1)

■ **Quiz 1:** The simple present tense + frequency adverbs.

Complete the sentences with the adverb of frequency and the correct form of the verb.

Examples: *(be, always)* My teacher ___*is always*___ friendly.

(write, often) I ___*often write*___ letters to my friends back home.

1. *(wake up, always)* Sam and Mary live in a small apartment. Sam _____
   _____ at 7:30 A.M.

2. *(get up, usually)* Mary _____ at the same time.

3. *(read, always)* They _____ the newspaper at breakfast.

4. *(leave, alway)* Sam works for a large company. He _____
   the house at 8:30 A.M.

5. *(drive, never)* Sam _____ his car to work. He likes to walk
   to his office.

6. *(drive, always)* Mary is a dentist. She _____ to work. She
   finishes work at 5:00 P.M. every day.

7. *(eat, seldom)* Sam and Mary _____ in restaurants. They
   like to cook at home.

8. *(be, never)* Sam's cousin, Roberto, is from Spain. He goes to English classes
   every morning. He _____ late for class.

9. *(write, usually)* Roberto _____ letters home several times
   a month.

10. *(think, often)* He _____ about his good friends in Spain.

■ **Quiz 2:** HAVE/HAS; DO/DOES; GO/GOES.

Cross out the error and write the correct word above the line.

have
Example: I ~~has~~ dinner with Maria twice a week.

1. Pablo and Ali do her homework together every evening.

2. I go to work at 8:00 A.M. My husband go at 9:00 A.M.

3. We often go to museums with ours friends.

4. Anna have lunch with her mother on Tuesday afternoons.

5. John and her wife always have breakfast together.

6. Carol and Paul goes downtown every day.

7. Tom always have a snack at 10 P.M.

8. Mr. and Mrs. Rice has two sons.

9. Anita has a new dress. His dress is red and white.

10. I does my work.

■ **Quiz 3:** YES/NO questions using DO/DOES and negatives.

Create questions and answers based on the cues. Your teacher will give you the name of a classmate for each question. Your answers may be positive or negative.

Example: go to English class every day (_____ *Marco* _____)

      A: Does Marco go to English class every day?

      B: Yes, he does. *or* No, he doesn't.

1. has curly hair (_____)

    A: _____

    B: _____

2. is in class today (_____)

    A: _____

    B: _____

3. speaks English fluently (_____)

    A: _____

    B: _____

4. has a good sense of humor (_____)

    A: _____

    B: _____

5. lives near the school (_____)

    A: _____

    B: _____

■ **Quiz 4:** Information questions.

Write a question for each answer.

Example: **A:** _____*Where do you live?*_____

B: On Central Street. (I live on Central Street.)

1. **A:** _____
   B: Cairo, Egypt. (I am from Cairo, Egypt.)

2. **A:** _____
   B: In an office. (I work in an office.)

3. **A:** _____
   B: At 9:00 A.M. (My morning classes begin at 9:00 A.M.)

4. **A:** _____
   B: Between 1:00 and 2:00 P.M. (I usually have lunch between 1:00 and 2:00 P.M.)

5. **A:** _____
   B: At 8:00 P.M. (The movie starts at 8:00 P.M.)

■ **Quiz 5:** Dictation.

Your teacher will read a paragraph about weekly activities. Write down the sentences on the lines below.

_____

_____

_____

_____

_____

_____

_____

_____

_____

■ **Quiz 6:** IT (time).

Write sentences telling the time in each city.

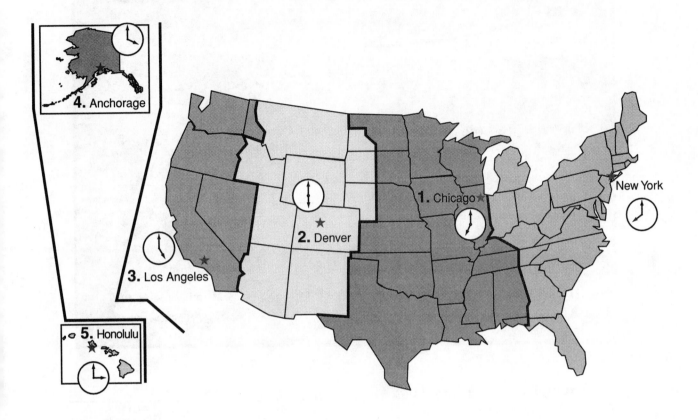

Example: ___*It is 8:00 p.m. in New York now.*_____

1. _____

2. _____

3. _____

4. _____

5. _____

■ **Quiz 7:** IT (weather).

Write sentences about today's weather. Use the weather map below.

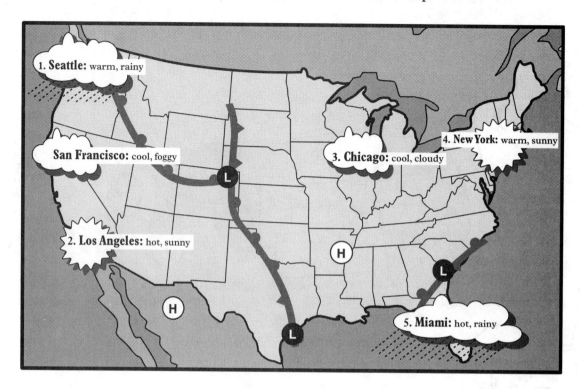

Example: _____It is cool and foggy in San Francisco today._____

1. _____

2. _____

3. _____

4. _____

5. _____

■ CHAPTER 2 TEST

A. Write a question for each answer, using the cues in parentheses.

Example: **A:** _____*Do you love baseball?*_____

B: Yes, I do. (I love baseball.)

1. **A:** _____

   B: On 12th Street. (Samir lives on 12th Street.)

2. **A:** _____

   B: No, I don't. (I don't like ice cream.)

3. **A:** _____

   B: It's November 17th. (The date today is November 17th.)

4. **A:** _____

   B: It's warm and sunny. (The weather is warm and sunny today.)

5. **A:** _____

   B: Yes, it is. (Chicago is usually cold in the winter.)

6. **A:** _____

   B: Yes, I am. (I am a doctor.)

7. **A:** _____

   B: At 12:30. (We usually eat lunch at 12:30.)

8. **A:** _____

   B: At 8:00 P.M. (The movie begins at 8:00 P.M.)

9. **A:** _____

   B: At 3:00 A.M. (The plane arrives at 3:00 A.M.)

10. **A:** _____

    B: My uncle. (That man is my uncle.)

B. Write a sentence for each verb. Use the adverbs *always, sometimes, seldom, often,* *usually,* and *rarely*.

Example: <u>   I always buy my lunch in the school cafeteria on Monday.   </u>

1. (*drink*) _____

2. (*buy*) _____

3. (*listen to*) _____

4. (*read*) _____

5. (*wake up*) _____

C. Each sentence has one error. Cross out the error and write the correct word above the line.

1. It has 6:00 P.M.

2. Anita works in home.

3. Ken meet me every Sunday for dinner and a movie.

4. We usually have lunch at 12:00 P.M. to 1:00 P.M.

5. The department stores open in Mondays at 10:00 A.M.

6. My pants is under my bed.

7. The glasses are on to the table.

8. It cloudy today.

9. It doesn't warm in Chicago in the winter.

10. We no see you in class anymore.

CHAPTER 3
Expressing Present Time (Part 2)

■ **Quiz 1:** **The present progressive.**

Your teacher will hand out pieces of paper with verbs written on them, and will ask students to act out the verbs for the class. Write down sentences which describe what each student is acting out.

_____

_____

_____

_____

_____

_____

_____

_____

_____

_____

_____

_____

_____

■ **Quiz 2:**   Using the present progressive.

Write a question about the cartoon strip for each answer. Use **where**, **what**, and **why**.

Example: **A:** _____*What is the man wearing?*_____
   B: The man is wearing a suit.

1. **A:** _____
   B: The man is sitting in a restaurant.

2. **A:** _____
   B: Because the food is cold. (The man is calling the waiter because the food is cold.)

3. **A:** _____
   B: To the kitchen. (The waiter is going into the kitchen.)

4. **A:** _____
   B: The waiter is bringing him hot food. (The man is happy because the waiter is bringing him hot food.)

5. **A:** _____
   B: A plate of pasta and meatballs. (The man is eating a plate of pasta and meatballs.)

■ **Quiz 3:**   Simple present vs. present progressive.

Choose the best answers to complete the sentences.

Example: Mary ___C___ two newspapers every day.
   A. read   B. is reading   C. reads

1. This morning, she _____ quickly because she is late.
   A. read   B. is reading   C. reads

2. My parents usually _____ me once a week on Sunday morning.
   A. call   B. are calling   C. calls

3. It is 10:00 A.M. The phone is ringing. I think that my parents _____ me right now.
   A. call   B. calls   C. are calling

4. Alex and Tina are married. They _____ dinner together every night.
   A. has   B. have   C. are having

5. Tina usually cooks, but tonight Alex _____.
   A. cooks   B. cook   C. is cooking

6. Mike _____ tennis with his friend, Ali, every Tuesday evening.
     A. plays   B. play   C. is playing

7. Ali usually _____, but today Mike _____.
     A. wins, wins   B. is winning, wins   C. wins, is winning

8. Our class _____ a quiz now.
     A. takes   B. is taking   C. take

9. Jean is very busy right now. She _____ some letters.
     A. write   B. is writing   C. writes

10. Paul _____ to school every day.
     A. walks   B. is walking   C. walk

■ **Quiz 4:** **Nonaction verbs.**

Complete the sentences. Use the SIMPLE PRESENT or the PRESENT PROGRESSIVE form. You may use a verb more than once.

wait	smell	cook	love

1. Peter ____*loves*____ tomatoes. He _____ with them all the time.

   Tonight he _____ dinner for his friends. His friends are very

   happy. They _____ in the living room and talking. The food

   _____ wonderful.

sing	hear	know	think

2. **A:** Shh! I _____ a noise!

   B: What is it?

   A: I don't _____. I _____ that someone is yelling.

   B: Oh! That's my neighbor! He _____ in the shower!

| be | look | sit | see |

3. **A:** Wow! _____ you _____ that?

   B: What _____ you _____ at?

   A: That beautiful bird. It _____ in that tree. It _____ yellow and black.

   B: I _____ a lot of trees, but I can't see any birds.

■ **Quiz 5:** NEED and WANT, WOULD LIKE, THINK ABOUT, and THINK THAT.

Complete the questions and sentences with your own words.

1. Would you like _____?

2. I think that _____.

3. Do you like _____?

4. Most people need _____.

5. Most people want _____.

6. _____ thinks that _____.

7. _____ think about _____.

8. _____ wants _____.

9. Do _____ like _____?

10. Do you think that _____?

■ Quiz 6:   THERE + BE statements and questions.

Look at the map of Coraltown. Complete the questions with the correct form of *be*.
Then, answer the questions.

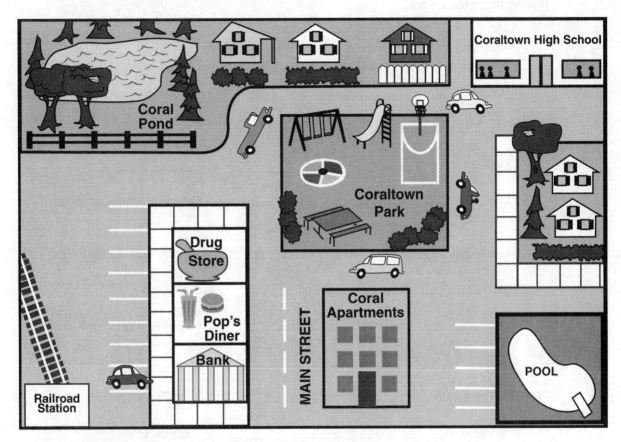

Example: **A:** _____ *Is* _____ there a playground in Coraltown?
            B: _____ *Yes, there is.* _____

1. **A:** _____ there a pond in Coraltown?

   B: _____

2. **A:** _____ there any apartment buildings in Coraltown?

   B: _____

3. **A:** _____ there a swimming pool in Coraltown?

   B: _____

4. **A:** _____ there any tennis courts in Coraltown?

   B: _____

5. **A:** _____ there an airport in Coraltown?

   B: _____

■ **Quiz 7:** Prepositions of location.

Look at the map of Coraltown again. Then complete the sentences with a preposition or phrase from the list and the correct form of *be*. You may use the same preposition or phrase more than once.

around	*inside*	*next to*
between	*in the middle of*	*on*
far away from	*near*	

Example: Coraltown Park _____ *is in the middle of* _____ town.

1. There _____ cars _____ Coraltown Park.

2. There _____ houses _____ the high school and the swimming pool.

3. Pop's Diner _____ the Coral Apartments.

4. There _____ trees _____ Coral Pond.

5. There _____ students _____ Coraltown High School.

6. The railroad station _____ the high school.

7. The drug store _____ Pop's Diner.

8. Pop's Diner _____ Main Street.

9. The swimming pool _____ Coral Pond.

10. The pond _____ a lot of trees.

■ CHAPTER 3 TEST

A. Complete the sentences with the best answer.

1. Yoko and Alex are in the library now. They _____.
   A. read   B. reads   C. are reading

2. The actors are happy. The show is ending. The people _____.
   A. clap   B. are clapping   C. claps

3. I always _____ English with my children. I want them to speak English well.
   A. am speaking   B. speaks   C. speak

4. Please don't talk to me now. I _____ about something.
   A. think   B. thinks   C. am thinking

5. Take an umbrella. It _____ outside.
   A. rain   B. is raining   C. are raining

6. What _____?
   A. he is wearing   B. he wears   C. is he wearing

7. Shh. I _____ a noise.
   A. hears   B. hear   C. am hearing

8. Tony _____ coffee. He wants tea.
   A. don't want   B. isn't wanting   C. doesn't want

9. We often _____ to discuss business at Ahmed's house.
   A. are meeting   B. meets   C. meet

10. I _____ a letter to my cousin now.
    A. write   B. writes   C. am writing

B. Write a question for each answer, using the cues in parentheses.

1. **A:** _____
   B: Yes, I would. (I would like some coffee.)

2. **A:** _____
   B: No, I don't. (I don't think that English grammar is difficult.)

3. **A:** _____
   B: Yes, I do. (I need a new car.)

4. **A:** _____
   B: Yes, there are. (There are many students in this school.)

5. **A:** _____
   B: Yes, it does. (It often rains in the winter in the United States.)

6. **A:** _____
   B: No, I don't. (I don't smell smoke.)

7. **A:** _____
   B: Yes, they do. (Bananas taste sweet.)

8. **A:** _____
   B: Yes, I am. (I'm taking an exam.)

9. **A:** _____
   B: Home. (I'm going home.)

10. **A:** _____
    B: Yes, I am. (I'm happy.)

C. Look at the picture. People are sightseeing in a tour boat. Complete each sentence with a phrase from the list.

in front of	*in the front of*	*in the middle of*
in back of	*in the back of*	*next to*

.

1. Gina and Bob are _____ Mary.

2. Ricardo is _____ the tour boat.

3. Mary, Gina, and Bob are _____ the tour boat.

4. Tom is _____ the tour boat.

5. Bob is sitting _____ Gina.

6. Tom is sitting _____ Gina.

7. The large boat is _____ the small boat.

8. Gina and Bob are sitting _____ Tom.

9. John is sitting _____ the small boat.

10. Ricardo is sitting _____ Mary, Bob, Gina, and Tom.

CHAPTER 4
Nouns and Pronouns

■ **Quiz 1:** Subjects and objects; adjective + noun.

In each sentence, underline the nouns. If a noun is used as the subject of the sentence, write **s** above it. If it is used as the object of the verb, write **ov** above it. If it is used as the object of a preposition, write **op** above it. Then (circle) the adjectives.

Example: The (hungry) girl has a (ripe) banana.

1. The young man is wearing a new suit.

2. Carla is watching an interesting movie on television.

3. You like dark colors, but I like light colors.

4. Mr. and Mrs. Smith usually eat fresh fish for dinner on Tuesdays.

5. Michael drives an old car to his office.

6. Tom has a brown dog.

7. Yoko is writing a long letter to her parents.

8. Young girls often play with dolls.

9. This expensive pen belongs to Martha.

10. I don't have your new address.

■ **Quiz 2:** Subject and object pronouns.

Complete the sentences, using the correct pronouns.

Example: **A:** Maria, is that _____*your*_____ shopping bag?

B: No, _____*it*_____ isn't. It's Sam's.

1. **A:** Who is that beautiful woman? Do you know _____?

   B: Yes, I do. I also know the man next to her. _____ is her husband!

2. Alan has coffee every morning. He likes _____ with milk and sugar.
   Rita likes her coffee black.

3. I live in a small white house on Main Street. _____ has five rooms. My two

   sons live in one bedroom. _____ usually play outside all day on the weekends.

   I help _____ with their homework every night.

4. **A:** How is your friend Carlos? Do you see _____ often?

   B: I usually see _____ once a week. We go to the gym together to work out.

5. We live close to my parents. They have dinner with _____ once a week. We

   are always happy to see _____ .

■ **Quiz 3:** Plural nouns.

List eight plural nouns for each category.

Animals and Insects	Things you eat and drink	Expensive things you can buy
pigs	*bananas*	*cars*

■ **Quiz 4:** Irregular plurals.

Write five sentences describing the picture.

Example: ___Two women are walking in the park._____

_____

_____

_____

_____

_____

_____

_____

_____

_____

_____

_____

■ **Quiz 5:** Count and noncount.

Correct the noun errors, if any.

1. Most country would like to have peace.

2. We get homeworks every day in this class.

3. How much tomatoes do you need?

4. Hiroko needs some advices about her schedule.

5. Mary's jewelry looks expensive, but it isn't.

6. Tony doesn't eat meat. He eats a lot of vegetable.

7. There is a lot of traffics in the city today.

8. The secretary has informations about our company. Please call her.

9. Teenagers like to play music loudly.

10. I hope you have good luck.

■ Quiz 6: A/AN and SOME; units of measure.

You would like to cook one of your country's favorite meals for your classmates. Write a shopping list of at least ten things you will need. Tell what amount of each thing you will need. Use a unit of measure for each thing.

Example: _____*A pound of rice.*_____

_____*A can of peas.*_____

1. _____

2. _____

3. _____

4. _____

5. _____

6. _____

7. _____

8. _____

9. _____

10. _____

■ **Quiz 7:** THE and Ø.

Fill in the blanks. Use *the* if it is needed. If it is not needed, write **Ø**.

Example: I need to buy ___Ø___ cheese.

1. _____ milk in my refrigerator is spoiled. I need to buy some more.

2. _____ oranges grow in Florida and California.

3. Some people think that _____ television is harmful for children.

4. _____ television in my living room is broken.

5. _____ men in this class are intelligent and hardworking.

6. _____ baseball is a very interesting game.

7. Teenagers like to listen to _____ music.

8. Teenagers in my neighborhood usually have _____ jobs in _____ afternoon.

9. I think I need _____ glasses. I can't see the blackboard clearly.

10. _____ diamond rings are expensive.

■ **Quiz 8:** Indefinite pronouns.

Choose the best answers to complete the sentences.

1. I gave Olga _____ for her birthday.
   a. anyone   b. something   c. anything

2. This week Bob is taking a vacation. He is fishing on the lake. He isn't calling

   _____ on the telephone.
   a. someone   b. any   c. anyone

3. The telephone is ringing. _____ is trying to call me.
   a. Anyone   b. Someone   c. Anybody

4. You can tell me your age. I won't tell _____.
   a. anyone   b. somebody   c. someone

5. Mark went shopping, but he didn't buy _____.
   a. something   b. any   c. anything

■ CHAPTER 4 TEST

A. Choose the best answers to complete the sentences.

1. Little children drink a lot of _____.
   a. the milk   b. milk   c. milks

2. Mr. Anderson is a doctor. _____ works at North Medical Center.
   a. His   b. He   c. He's

3. I don't know _____ about computers.
   a. anything   b. nothing   c. no one

4. Ms. Hall has five students. She teaches _____ English twice a week.
   a. we   b. her   c. them

5. Can I call _____ at home about the project?
   a. you're   b. your   c. you

6. _____ is at home now. Please leave a message.
   a. Anyone   b. Nothing   c. No one

7. _____ is wonderful.
   a. The love   b. Love   c. Loves

8. Maria likes to listen to _____ when she does her homework.
   a. musics   b. the music   c. music

9. We have many friends in different countries. They send _____ letters and postcards from all over the world.
   a. we   b. us   c. him

10. Hiroko is reading a book. _____ is very interesting.
    a. It   b. Her   c. They

B. Complete each sentence with a noun from the list. If necessary, use the plural form.

city	*information*	*potato*
class	*knife*	*traffic*
furniture	*orange*	*woman*
homework		

1. _____ are dangerous for children to hold.

2. _____ grow in Florida and in other warm places.

3. Because of the car accident, there is a lot of _____ on Main Street.

4. You need five _____ in that recipe for French fries.

5. Mr. and Mrs. Rice have antique _____ in their living room. It is very beautiful.

6. All of my _____ are in the same school building.

7. How many _____ are there in your class?

8. Many people live in _____. Some people live in small towns.

9. Let's do our ESL _____ together at your house this evening.

10. The book has important _____ about this company.

C. <u>Underline</u> the nouns. If a noun is used as the subject of the sentence, write **s** above it. If it is used as the object of the verb, write **ov** above it. If it is used as the object of a preposition, write **op** above it. Then (circle) the adjectives.

1. A tall man is standing near the beach. He is a famous photographer. He is taking

   pictures of the people in the water. The people are waving at him.

2. Clara loves animals. She has two black cats, a large dog, and three bright yellow

   birds in her house. She plays with them after school.

3. Yoko had a surprise party last night for Laura's birthday. Yoko baked a delicious

   cake. She invited ten people to the party.

CHAPTER **5**
Expressing Past Time

■ **Quiz 1:**   Past tense of BE, questions, negatives.

Write a question for each answer, using the cues in parentheses.

Example: **A:** _____*Was your daughter at the library yesterday?*_____

   B: Yes, she was. (My daughter was at the library.)

1. **A:** _____
   B: No, I wasn't. (I wasn't at the gym on Thursday.)

2. **A:** _____
   B: Yes, I was. (I was at home yesterday.)

3. **A:** _____
   B: Yes, it was. (My trip was interesting.)

4. **A:** _____
   B: At the shopping mall. (I was at the shopping mall last night.)

5. **A:** _____
   B: No, he wasn't. He was at his son's house. (Carlos wasn't at the concert last night.)

■ **Quiz 2:**   Simple past tense; past time words.

Write sentences using the verbs and the past time words in parentheses.

Example: (*play, last week*)   _____*I played chess with James last week.*_____

1. (*be, two hours ago*) _____

2. (*snow, last winter*) _____

3. (*watch, yesterday evening*) _____

4. (*visit, yesterday morning*) _____

5. (*call, five minutes ago*) _____

■ **Quiz 3:** Irregular past tense verbs.

Complete the paragraph with the correct past tense forms of the irregular verbs. Use each verb only once.

drink	leave	ride
eat	put	see
get	read	think
✔ go		

Last night, Jim _____ *went* _____ to bed at midnight. This morning, he

_____ up at 6:30 A.M., shaved, and _____ on his clothes. He

_____ breakfast and _____ his apartment at 7:30 A.M. He

_____ the train to work. On the train, he _____ his good friend

Joe. At work, he _____ a cup of coffee and _____ his mail.

Then he _____ about all the work he had to do that day.

■ **Quiz 4:** Irregular past tense verbs; questions and negatives.

Write questions and short answers based on the cues.

Example: **A:** _____ *Did you take an English class last year?* _____

B: _____ *No, I didn't.* _____ (I didn't take an English class last year.)

1. **A:** _____

   B: _____ (I didn't see Helen yesterday morning.)

2. **A:** _____

   B: _____ (I slept on the plane.)

3. **A:** _____

   B: _____ (I didn't go to the library.)

4. **A:** _____

   B: _____ (Marco didn't write this composition.)

5. **A:** _____

   B: _____ (We ate lunch at Sam's house.)

■ **Quiz 5:**   **WH-questions.**

Match the questions to the answers.

_c_   1. Where is the bus stop?

____   2. What time did you wake up this morning?

____   3. Why did you take this class?

____   4. When did you meet your husband?

____   5. Where did you buy your camera?

a. In an electronics store.

b. In June.

c. Down the street.

d. At 7:30 A.M.

e. Because I want to learn English and get a better job

■ **Quiz 6:**   **WHAT and WHO questions.**

Write questions beginning with **what** or **who** based on the cues.

Example: **A:** _____ *Who cooked the dinner?* _____
          B: Aunt Sara.

1. **A:** _____
   B: My mother.

2. **A:** _____
   B: A movie.

3. **A:** _____
   B: A new bicycle.

4. **A:** _____
   B: I did.

5. **A:** _____
   B: A sandwich.

6. **A:** _____
   B: A cup of coffee.

7. **A:** _____
   B: A suit.

8. **A:** _____
   B: My brother.

9. **A:** _____
   B: My English teacher.

10. **A:** _____
    B: My homework.

■ **Quiz 7:** Time clauses with BEFORE, AFTER, and WHEN.

Combine the two ideas into one sentence, using the given time word.

Example: (*after*) We drove for two hours. We stopped at a gas station.

_____*After we drove for two hours, we stopped at a gas station.*_____

1. (*after*) I ate lunch. I took a walk.

   _____

   _____

2. (*when*) Jane met her husband. She was twenty years old.

   _____

   _____

3. (*before*) I didn't speak English. I came to this country.

   _____

   _____

4. (*after*) He saw the fire. He called the fire department.

   _____

   _____

5. (*when*) Her parents left. The child started to cry.

   _____

   _____

■ CHAPTER 5 TEST

A. Write questions based on the cues.

1. **A:** _____
   B: Yes, I was. (I was at the party last night.)

2. **A:** _____
   B: No, I didn't. (I didn't do the homework assignment.)

3. **A:** _____
   B: To the gym. (I went to the gym last night.)

4. **A:** _____
   B: Because I had a headache. (I didn't call you yesterday because I had a headache.)

5. **A:** _____
   B: My uncle. (My uncle took me out to dinner yesterday.)

6. **A:** _____
   B: No, I didn't. (I didn't take the exam.)

7. **A:** _____
   B: Before I left home. (I had breakfast before I left home.)

8. **A:** _____
   B: It means "sick." (It means "ill.")

9. **A:** _____
   B: Yes, it was. (The play was interesting.)

10. **A:** _____
    B: No, it didn't. (It didn't snow yesterday evening.)

B. Write a paragraph with six sentences about what you did yesterday. Use the verbs in the list.

buy	listen to	see
eat	put	wake
go	ride	watch
have		

_____

_____

_____

_____

_____

_____

_____

_____

_____

_____

_____

_____

C. Correct the errors in each sentence. Some sentences may not have an error.

1. Tony goes to Ali's house last night. _____

2. Mariko called Tina yesterday night about the homework assignment.

3. Where you were yesterday afternoon?

4. I readed an interesting book when I was on vacation.

5. Tim come to this country after he finished high school.

6. Kim was watch a funny television show last week.

7. Did Frank met Pablo at the airport yesterday?

8. We brought a delicious cake to the party.

9. I drinked a cup of coffee before work.

10. I was happy to see you last week.

Midterm Exam

A. Choose the best answer.

1. Dogs and horses _____.
   a. are animals   b. is an animal   c. isn't animal

2. Mrs. Rice _____ a student. She's a teacher.
   a. is   b. aren't   c. isn't

3. Carlos was _____ yesterday.
   a. in home   b. on home   c. at home

4. Are those _____ books?
   a. yours   b. you   c. your

5. Kate is wearing a suit. _____ suit is dark blue.
   a. Their   b. Her   c. Hers

6. **A:** Where's your notebook?

   B: _____ in my bag.
   a. It's   b. Its   c. Is

7. _____ watch is new.
   a. I   b. My   c. I have a

8. Mr. Rice _____ a small dog.
   a. have   b. is having   c. has

9. _____ to class on time.
   a. Always Sam come   c. Sam always comes
   b. Sam comes always

10. My husband and I usually _____ dinner at 6:00 P.M.
    a. eats   b. are eating   c. eat

11. Albert _____ for dinner.
    a. is ever late   b. is never late   c. is late never

12. Yoko and Jack _____ their homework together every week.
    a. does   b. are doing   c. do

13. Pablo _____ to the gym every Sunday.
    a. go   b. is going   c. goes

14. Sue _____ like black coffee. She likes coffee with milk and sugar.
    a. don't   b. doesn't   c. isn't

15. **A:** _____ you usually get up in the morning?

    B: At 7:30.
    a. What time are   b. What time does   c. What time do

16. **A:** How's the weather today?

    B: _____ rainy.
    a. Its   b. It   c. It's

17. **A:** What are you wearing today?

    B: _____ a green dress.
    a. You're wearing   b. I'm wearing   c. I wear

18. **A:** What _____ doing?

    B: They're reading the newspaper.
    a. is he   b. do they   c. are they

19. **A:** Is Hiroko sleeping?

    B: _____ .
    a. Yes, I do   b. No, she doesn't   c. No, she isn't

20. I walk to work everyday. I _____ my car.
    a. am not taking   b. doesn't take   c. don't take

21. _____ the teacher's directions?
    a. Did you understand   c. Did you understood
    b. Were you understanding

22. **A:** What are you doing right now?

    B: I'm _____ a concert on the radio.
    a. hearing   b. listen to   c. listening to

23. _____ something to drink?
    a. Would like   b. Would you like   c. Do you like

24. Alex _____ his rent is too expensive.
    a. thinks about   b. thinks that   c. thinks what

25. How _____ in this classroom?
    a. are many students   c. many students are there
    b. many students there are

26. Pedro has a new car. He bought _____ last Friday.
    a. it's   b. its   c. it

27. Michael and Susan have two _____.
    a. child   b. childrens   c. children

28. Kyoung Sun called the school office for _____.
    a. informations   c. an information
    b. some information

29. Can I have _____ apple?
    a. an   b. a   c. some

30. _____ book belongs to Roberto.
    a. Those   b. This   c. These

31. I don't know _____ about that subject.
    a. nothing   b. any   c. anything

32. My parents live on your street. Do you know _____?
    a. they're   b. them   c. their

33. Last night, Ellen _____ a delicious meal.
    a. was cook   b. was cooked   c. cooked

34. I'm so happy. It finally _____ raining.
    a. was stop   b. stopped   c. was stopped

35. After Yumiko _____ the letter, she sent it.
    a. writes   b. wrote   c. was wrote

36. Rita saw me _____.
    a. was two weeks   c. two weeks ago
    b. before two weeks

37. Were you home _____?
    a. last night   b. last morning   c. last afternoon

38. Sam lives _____ the United States.
    a. on   b. at   c. in

39. Mr. Smith lives _____ 14 Brook Road.
    a. on   b. in   c. at

40. Does your uncle live _____ Main Street?
    a. in   b. at   c. on

B. Choose the best answer based on the picture cues.

41. The painting is _____ the table.
    a. below   b. on   c. above

42. The apples are _____ the basket.
    a. in   b. on   c. next to

43. The bottle is _____ the basket.
    a. under   b. next to   c. in

44. The ball is _____ the table.
    a. between   b. on   c. under

45. The dog is _____ the ball and the chair.
    a. under   b. behind   c. between

46. Susan is sitting _____ the row.
    a. in front of   b. in the middle of   c. on top of

47. Mark is sitting _____ of Susan.
    a. in back of   b. back of   c. around

48. The teacher is standing _____ the class.
    a. in front of   b. behind   c. on

49. John is sitting _____ the blackboard.
    a. behind   b. far away from   c. in front of

50. Alex is waiting _____ the classroom.
    a. inside   b. behind   c. outside

C. Write ten sentences about two students in your class. You may include age, **appearance,** family, job, home, and place of birth.

_____

_____

_____

_____

_____

_____

_____

_____

_____

_____

_____

_____

CHAPTER 6
Expressing Future Time

■ **Quiz 1:** BE GOING TO.

Look at the Monday schedules for Mr. and Mrs. Rice. Complete the sentences. Use **be going to** and an appropriate verb.

DAILY PLANNER FOR *Alan Rice*

Monday

9 – 10 A.M.	Meeting with Mr. King
10 – 11 A.M.	Dictate letters to secretary
12:30 – 1:30 P.M.	Lunch with Clara
2 – 4 P.M.	Work on report
8 – 9 P.M.	Tennis with Bob
11 P.M.	Watch television news

DAILY PLANNER FOR *Clara Rice*

Monday

9 – 10 A.M.	Teach English class
12:30 – 1:30 P.M.	Lunch with Alan
2 – 5 P.M.	See students
5:30 P.M.	Dentist appointment
8 – 9 P.M.	Prepare lecture for tomorrow

Example: At 11 P.M., Alan Rice ___*is going to watch*___ the news on television.

1. Alan Rice works in a bank. On Monday morning, he _____

   with Mr. King. At 11 A.M., he _____ his secretary.

   He _____ lunch with his wife, Clara, between 12:30 and

   1:30 P.M. In the afternoon, he _____ on a report. After

   work, he _____ tennis with his friend Bob.

2. Clara Rice is an English professor at Jones College. On Monday morning, she

   _____ a class. After that, she _____

   her husband for lunch. Between 2:00 and 5:00 P.M., she _____

   students in her office. At 5:30 P.M., she _____ to the dentist.

   In the evening, she _____ a lecture for Wednesday's class.

■ **Quiz 2:** Future and past time words.

Write pairs of sentences using the PAST TIME and FUTURE TIME words.

Example: last night / tomorrow night

_____*I had dinner with my parents last night.*_____

_____*I'm going to have dinner with my teacher tomorrow night.*_____

1. yesterday / tomorrow

   A: _____

   B: _____

2. last Sunday / next Sunday

   A: _____

   B: _____

3. one hour ago / in one hour

   A: _____

   B: _____

4. a couple of months ago / in a couple of months

   A: _____

   B: _____

5. yesterday morning / this morning

   A: _____

   B: _____

■ **Quiz 3:** WILL.

Use the picture cues to complete the sentences about the future. Use **will**.

Example: Susan _____*will eat*_____ dinner with her husband tomorrow evening.

1. Ricardo and Laura _____ tomorrow at 5:00 P.M. After the

    wedding, they _____ good-bye to their friends and families. They

    _____ for their honeymoon in Europe the next day.

2. On Sunday afternoon, Bing _____ his car. After that, he

    _____ 20 miles to his parents' house in the country.

■ **Quiz 4:** Future tense questions.

Write five questions that ask a student in your class about his or her plans for the weekend.

Example: _Are you going to stay home on Friday evening?_

1. _____

2. _____

3. _____

4. _____

5. _____

■ **Quiz 5:** MAY, MIGHT, and MAYBE.

Complete the sentences with **maybe, may,** or **might.** If both **may** and **might** are correct, write **may/might.**

Example: Our class ____ _may/might_ ____ take a trip to an art museum next week.

1. It _____ snow tomorrow. Do you have boots and a heavy jacket?

2. _____ Juan will meet me for dinner this evening.

3. I'm very nervous. _____ I won't pass the exam.

4. **A:** Is Anita going to come to the baseball game tonight?

   B: I don't know. She _____.

5. **A:** Where are you going to go on your vacation?

   B: I'm not sure. We _____ go skiing in Colorado.

6. **A:** Is Hiroko going to wear her red suit to the job interview?

   B: She _____.

7. **A:** What are you going to buy your wife for her birthday?

   B: I don't know. _____ I'll buy her a beautiful ring.

8. **A:** What happened to Abdullah? Why isn't he here?

   B: _____ he's ill.

9. After I finish my bachelor's degree, I _____ apply to **graduate school.**

10. _____ Alex won't come tonight. He is very busy.

■ **Quiz 6:** Future time clauses with BEFORE, AFTER, and WHEN.

Write five sentences about your plans for today, using *before, after,* and *when* and the words in parentheses. Use the FUTURE TENSE or *may/might.*

Example: (after, finish class) *After I finish class, I'm going to have lunch.* _____

1. (after, have a break) _____

_____

2. (when, get home) _____

_____

3. (before, eat dinner) _____

_____

4. (after, finish dinner) _____

_____

5. (before, go to bed) _____

_____

■ **Quiz 7:** IF-clauses in future and habitual present.

Complete the sentences with your own words.

Example: If the teacher is absent tomorrow, ____*I will study in the library.*____

1. If it rains tomorrow, _____.

2. If I learn to speak English very well, _____.

3. I will _____ if I _____.

4. If I have time tonight, I _____.

5. If I have enough money, I usually _____.

■ CHAPTER 6 TEST

A. Complete the sentences with the best answer.

1. If the weather _____ nice tomorrow, I will work outside in the garden.
   - a. is going to be
   - b. will be
   - c. is

2. Gary wasn't in class _____ morning. He was sick.
   - a. last
   - b. tomorrow
   - c. yesterday

3. Mr. Johnson will see you _____.
   - a. a few minutes ago
   - b. an hour ago
   - c. in a few minutes

4. Rossini's Cafe will open _____.
   - a. in two more weeks
   - b. two weeks ago
   - c. 10 more minutes

5. Ricardo and Maria _____ come to the party. They will decide tomorrow and call you.
   - a. maybe
   - b. may
   - c. might be

6. What _____ going to wear to Frank's wedding?
   - a. will you
   - b. are you
   - c. you are

7. Before _____ to class, Ayumi usually buys a cup of coffee and a sandwich.
   - a. she is coming
   - b. she's coming
   - c. she comes

8. _____ I got dressed, I took a hot shower.
   - a. Before
   - b. When
   - c. After

9. _____ going to be late again?
   - a. Are they
   - b. Will they
   - c. They might

10. _____ at work tomorrow?
    - a. Will be
    - b. Will you be
    - c. Were you

B. Write a paragraph of five sentences about some things you are going to do this week. Use **be going to** and **will**. You may also use **before, after, when,** and *if*-clauses.

Example: _____*If I finish my homework tonight, I will visit my friends at*_____

_____*their apartment.*_____

_____

_____

_____

_____

_____

_____

_____

_____

_____

_____

_____

_____

_____

_____

_____

C. Correct the errors in each sentence.

1. What you do on Friday evenings?

2. Right now, we write an exam.

3. I maybe play tennis with Susan tomorrow evening.

4. **A:** Will Fred be at the party?

    B: No, he isn't.

5. Jake is go to the gym now.

6. I will going to meet you before class tomorrow.

7. **A:** Will you be at the library later?

    B: I maybe.

8. We won't to see each other tomorrow. I will be out of town.

9. Is Max and James going to work together on the report?

10. We will meet one week ago.

CHAPTER 7
Expressing Ability

■ **Quiz 1:**   CAN, KNOW HOW TO, and COULD.

Complete the dialogues with **can, know how to,** or **could** in the positive or negative form.

Example: **A:** _____*Can*_____ you count to ten in Portuguese?

   B: No, I _____*can't.*_____

1. **A:** Mike, do you _____ multiply and divide?

   B: Yes, I do if I use my calculator.

   A: _____ you tell me the answer to question 7?

   B: No, I _____. I _____ do the homework because my

   calculator was broken.

2. **A:** I wanted to invite Tina to the party, but I _____ reach her. Her

   telephone was busy all night.

   B: _____ you try her again today?

3. **A:** Do you _____ fix a flat tire?

   B: Yes, I do.

   A: Well, I think I need your help. I have a flat.

4. **A:** _____ you read the bottom line of the eye chart?

   B: No, I _____. The print is too small for me.

5. **A:** _____ you speak English fluently?

   B: Yes, of course.

■ **Quiz 2:** VERY, TOO, TOO MUCH, and TOO MANY.

Correct the error in each sentence.

Example: I am too ~~much~~ heavy. I am going to go on a diet.

1. This dress is too much small, so I can't wear it.

2. Ricardo can afford the car because it's too expensive.

3. Joe has too many work to do. He can't speak with you now.

4. The size of our class is perfect. There aren't too much people.

5. I feel too tired. I'd like to go to sleep now.

■ **Quiz 3:** TOO + adjective, adjective + ENOUGH, and ENOUGH.

Use the picture cues to complete the sentences.

Example: This homework is ___*too*___

___*difficult*___ to do.

1. I burned my mouth! This soup is

_____ to eat.

2. Mr. Rice can't buy the car. It's

_____ for

him. He doesn't have _____

_____ to buy it now.

3. John is _____ to go to high school.

   He's not even _____ for elementary

   school.

4. If Susan has _____,

   she will eat lunch. She was _____

   _____ to eat lunch yesterday.

5. This suitcase is _____

   for me to lift. Can you help me? I'm not

   _____ to lift it.

6. **A:** Would you like some dessert?

   B: No, thank you. I'm _____

   _____ to eat another bite.

■ **Quiz 4:** BE ABLE TO; polite questions.

    A. Write polite questions based on the situations.

        Example: Your friend has a watch. You would like to know the time.
               Excuse me. Can you tell me what time it is?

      1. Your friend has an electronic dictionary. You would like to borrow it.

        _____

      2. It is very hot in the room. You would like someone to open a window.

        _____

      3. You want your friend to tell you what yesterday's homework was.

        _____

      4. You would like to offer a guest in your house a cup of coffee.

        _____

      5. You would like your roommate to turn down the music. It's too loud.

        _____

    B. For each word, write one thing it can do. Use **be able to**.

        Example: a car   *A car is able to go very fast.*

        1. a fish   _____

        2. a bird   _____

        3. a baby   _____

        4. a computer _____

        5. you   _____

■ **Quiz 5:** Imperatives.

    A. Match the sentences.

      ____ 1. Knock, knock.   a. Take two aspirin and go to sleep.

      ____ 2. Hurry up!   b. Please hang up your clothes.

      ____ 3. I have a headache. I think I have fever.   c. Sure. Please have a seat.

      ____ 4. This room is a mess!   d. Come in.

      ____ 5. Can I speak with you for a minute?   e. We're going to be late.

B. Create an imperative sentence for each situation.

1. Your son, a teenager, is going skiing for the first time. You are worried about him.

   You say: _____

2. Someone has opened a window in your office. A cold wind is blowing into the room.

   You say: _____

3. Someone asks you for directions to the bank. It is two blocks away, at 14th Street.

   You say: _____

4. You are walking down the street. You see someone stealing another person's briefcase.

   You (shouting): _____

■ **Quiz 6:** **AT and IN for location.**

Complete the sentences with *at* or *in*.

Example: **A:** Where is Max?
              B: He's ___*at*___ work.

1. **A:** Can you please pick me up? I'm _____ the station.

   B: Sure. Please wait _____ the waiting room. I'll look for you there.

2. I can't find my keys. I know they're somewhere _____ this house!

3. Laura is _____ home. Please call her there.

4. I was very sick yesterday. I was _____ bed all day.

5. Dangerous criminals belong _____ prison.

6. I'm _____ my office now. Let's meet _____ school tomorrow to discuss the

   homework.

7. Kim wasn't _____ class last week. She was _____ Florida on vacation.

■ CHAPTER 7 TEST

A. Complete the sentences with the best answer.

1. This door is locked. I don't _____ open it. Please help me.
    a. can   b. know how to   c. know to

2. Yoko and Mark _____ to attend class yesterday. They missed their train.
    a. weren't able   b. couldn't   c. can't

3. This desk is _____ for me to lift. Could you help me move it?
    a. to heavy   b. too heavy   c. heavy enough

4. **A:** _____ like some ice cream?

   B: Of course!
    a. Could you   b. Can you   c. Would you

5. Robert _____ play the accordion beautifully when he was a child.
    a. knows how to   b. can   c. could

6. It's _____ to go to the beach. I'll get our bathing suits and suntan lotion.
    a. very warm   b. too warm   c. warm enough

7. **A:** Can I speak with you for a few minutes?

   B: Sure, _____.
    a. please sit down   b. please to sit down   c. sitting down

8. James didn't _____ speak English at all before he came to the United States.
    a. know   b. knew   c. know how to

9. There are _____ people in this restaurant. Let's go to a quieter place.
    a. too much   b. very   c. too many

10. I'd like to stay home. I'm _____ to go out tonight.
    a. very tired   b. tired   c. too tired

B. Write a polite question to fit each answer.

1. **Waiter:** _____

   Customer: A hamburger and french fries, please.

2. **Host:** _____

   Guest: Yes, I'd love some coffee.

3. **Student:** _____

   Teacher: Yes, meet me in my office after class.

4. **Customer:** _____

   Supermarket employee: The carrots are in the produce section.

5. **Student:** _____

   Classmate: Sure, but please return it to me after class. It was a gift from my father.

C. Complete the sentences with *at* or *in*.

1. **A:** Where were you born?

   B: _____ Morocco.

2. **A:** Can I call you _____ home?

   B: Of course.

3. Hiroko is _____ work now. She'll be back later.

4. Dangerous criminals belong _____ jail.

5. Pablo is a bank teller. He works _____ the loan department of Coraltown Savings Bank.

CHAPTER 8
Nouns, Pronouns, and Adjectives

■ **Quiz 1:**   Noun and adjective modifiers; word order of adjectives.

Complete each sentence. Put the given nouns and adjectives in their correct order.
Punctuate correctly.

Example: (tea, green, hot)

I like to drink a cup of _____*hot green tea*_____ after dinner.

1. (restaurant, Italian, favorite)

   I took my friends to my _____.

2. (suit, blue, dark)

   You can wear the _____ to the classical music concert.

3. (house, big, white)

   Mr. and Mrs. Kelly live in the _____ down the street.

4. (vases, antique, glass)

   Mrs. Rice collects _____. It's her hobby.

5. (people, intelligent, young)

   We met some _____ at the party.

6. (paintings, large, colorful)

   The children painted many _____ in
   their art class.

7. (address book, black, small)

   I can't find my _____. Maybe I lost it.

8. (man, handsome, tall)

   A _____ asked me for a date.

9. (peaches, sweet, ripe)

   I love to eat _____ for desert.

10. (woman, serious, young)

   Martha is a _____. She would like to
   study medicine.

■ **Quiz 2:** Expressions of quantity; subject-verb agreement.

Complete the sentences with information from your own experience. Use the PRESENT TENSE.

Example: Some of _____*my friends drive*_____ .

1. None of _____.

2. All of _____.

3. Almost all of _____.

4. Most of _____.

5. One of _____.

■ **Quiz 3:** Possessive nouns and pronouns; WHOSE questions.

Correct the errors.

Example: That tall young man is Jack Smith. He is ~~mine~~ *my* friend.

1. Whose bag is that? It's Rita.

2. That coat is mine. It's not your.

3. Hiroko husband works for a large computer company.

4. Mark and Susan live in Colorado. They're house is in the Rocky Mountains.

5. Peggy isn't at home now, but shes sister is.

6. Ours class has many nice people.

7. Please give she the message.

8. That's my cousin. He's name is Sam.

9. His studying English at our college.

10. I bought a new suit and paid for its by check.

■ **Quiz 4:** Noun + conjunction + noun.

Complete the sentences with appropriate nouns.

Example: My favorite foods are ___*chocolate, chicken,*___ and ___*rice*___ .

1. You can buy _____, _____, and _____ at any supermarket.

2. _____ and _____ are major cities in Europe.

3. What would you like to drink? Would you like _____ or _____?

4. _____, _____, and _____ are animals.

5. I love to look at _____ and _____.

■ **Quiz 5:** Indirect objects with TO and FOR.

Arrange the sentence parts to form a correct sentence.

Example: some good news / Anna / told / her mother

___*Anna told her mother some good news.*___

1. a postcard my friends / sent / from Korea / me

_____

2. Can / lend / you / your dictionary / me

_____

3. Frank / new car / showed / us / his

_____

4. Minako / her dog / gave / a bath

_____

5. Sam / for his wife / opened / the door

_____

6. The mechanic / my car /fixed / for me

_____

7. The teacher / answered / for me / a question

_____

8. John / wrote / to his parents / a letter

_____

9. Maria / handed / to me / the book

_____

10. My wife / for me / a check / cashed

_____

■ **Quiz 6:** **Indirect objects with BUY, GET, and MAKE.**

Create sentences using the given cues.

Example: buy / father

_____ *I bought my father a beautiful watch for his birthday.* _____

1. buy / myself

_____

2. introduce / wife

_____

3. made / salad

_____

4. got / mother

_____

5. explain / student

_____

■ CHAPTER 8 TEST

A. Choose the best answer.

1. Mr. Rice introduced Sara to _____ man.
   - a. a young Italian
   - b. an Italian young
   - c. a young and Italian

2. I will wear my _____ suit to the business meeting tomorrow.
   - a. wool dark blue
   - b. blue dark wool
   - c. dark blue wool

3. _____ people like ice cream.
   - a. Almost
   - b. Most of
   - c. Most

4. _____ my friends speaks Mandarin Chinese fluently.
   - a. All of
   - b. One of
   - c. Most of

5. Mr. Alvarez owns that store. It belongs to _____.
   - a. him
   - b. his
   - c. he

6. Please pass _____ the salt.
   - a. to me
   - b. my
   - c. me

7. That's _____ briefcase, not mine.
   - a. John is
   - b. John's
   - c. Johns

8. _____ keys are these?
   - a. Whose
   - b. Who's
   - c. Who are

9. Frank made dinner _____.
   - a. to his wife
   - b. for her wife
   - c. for his wife

10. Yuko _____.
    - a. introduced to me her father
    - b. introduced me her father
    - c. introduced her father to me

B. For each noun, write a correct sentence. Use two adjectives or one adjective and a noun modifier.

    Example: house

                Mr. and Mrs. Jackson live in a yellow brick house.   OR

                Mr. and Mrs. Jackson live in an old yellow house.

1. (*suit*)

_____

2. (*movie*)

_____

3. (*sandwich*)

_____

4. (*hair*)

_____

5. (*eyes*)

_____

6. (*rose*)

_____

7. (*man*)

_____

8. (*woman*)

_____

9. (*painting*)

_____

10. (*bird*)

_____

C. Correct the pronoun errors.

George and Maria came to this country in May. Their came from Brazil. All of they family lives in Brazil. He is an intelligent young engineer. His studying English in a language school.

Maria is a children's dentist. Her is studying English reading, writing, and conversation with a private tutor. She's private tutor is American.

CHAPTER 9
Making Comparisons

■ Quiz 1:   THE SAME, SIMILAR, DIFFERENT, LIKE, and ALIKE.

Correct the errors, if any.

Example: My husband and I don't like *the* ^ same movies.

1. John's haircut is same as mine.

2. Hiroko and Minako are twins. They look like.

3. British English is different than American English in certain ways.

4. Are my homework answers similar with yours?

5. A motorcycle is alike a bicycle in some ways.

6. We signed up for this class at same time.

7. Jack's handwriting is similar his brother's.

8. English and Spanish are similar to in some ways, but different in other ways.

9. Love is alike a rose.

10. Marie and Jean come from same country.

■ Quiz 2:   -ER and MORE.

Complete the paragraphs, using the **-er** or **more** form of comparison.

Example: Skyscrapers are (*tall*) _____*taller*_____ than houses.

1. Rabbits and elephants are both animals. Rabbits are (*small*) _____

   than elephants and can run (*fast*) _____. Elephants are (*heavy*)

   _____ than rabbits and have (*long*) _____ noses.

2. Rita and Maria are sisters. Rita is (*old*) _____ and (*educated*)

   _____ than Maria. Rita is a banker, and Maria is a

   television news reporter. Maria is (*famous*) _____ than

   her sister. She is also (*funny*) _____. Rita is (*serious*)

   _____ and (*conservative*) _____

   than Maria.

■ Quiz 3:   AS . . . AS; LESS THAN.

Make sentences using **as . . . as** or **less than** with the items listed.

Example: (flower, tree, big)

   _____*A flower isn't as big as a tree.*_____

1. (silver, gold, expensive)

   _____

2. (grape juice, water, sweet)

   _____

3. (money, health, important)

   _____

4. (skydiving, walking, exciting)

   _____

5. (a rainbow, a cloud, colorful)

   _____

■ Quiz 4: Using BUT.

Match the columns.

_e_ 1. I can speak English,   a. but I can.

____ 2. Susan can't babysit for you tonight,   b. but her sister has black hair.

____ 3. Ed has a beautiful new car,   c. but his wife drinks tea.

____ 4. Laura has blonde hair,   d. but James doesn't.

____ 5. Mr. Rice drinks coffee every morning,   e. but not Spanish.

■ Quiz 5: ONE OF + superlative.

Make a sentence with each phrase plus **one of**. Change the adjective to the superlative.

Example: a happy person that I know

_____ *My friend Steve is one of the happiest people that I know.* _____

1. a good actor in the movies

_____

2. an important person in this country

_____

3. an expensive car

_____

4. an interesting person that I know

_____

5. a good place to take a vacation

_____

■ **Quiz 6:** Adjectives and adverbs.

(Circle) the adjectives and underline the adverbs and adverb phrases in the sentences.

Example: I can play the guitar underline{very well}.

That was a (great) movie!

1. Marco studies hard every evening.

2. Comics are very easy to read.

3. Please drive carefully.

4. Yumiko speaks English well.

5. You are speaking too quickly. Please speak more slowly.

6. We can meet tomorrow for an early lunch.

7. Clara buys clothes late in the season when they are on sale.

8. This coffee is very good!

9. That dress fits you perfectly.

10. Young Sam is a fast learner.

■ **Quiz 7:** **Comparisons with adverbs.**

Complete the sentences by using **as . . . as** or **more . . . than** and the adverb given.

Example: (*skillfully*) Mr. Robbins plays chess _____*more skillfully than*_____ any of
his friends.

1. (*beautifully*) Patrick is an opera singer. He sings _____
anyone I know.

2. (*hard*) My mother works _____ my father.

3. (*fluently*) Elizabeth speaks English _____ me.

4. (*well*) I can't play tennis _____ my tennis teacher.

5. (*quickly*) Please slow down. I can't walk _____ you.

6. (*often*) I like to practice my English _____ possible.

7. (*early*) The older children don't go to bed _____ their
baby sister.

8. (*neat*) Liza's handwriting is sloppy. She doesn't write _____
I do.

9. (*fast*) A turtle doesn't move _____ a rabbit.

10. (*careful*) Please let Sam drive us home. He drives _____
you.

■ CHAPTER 9 TEST

A. Choose the best answer.

1. Karen is _____ people I have met.
   a. more intelligent   b. most intelligent   c. one of the most intelligent

2. Great Britain is _____ Portugal.
   a. larger   b. as large   c. larger than

3. Michael is _____ person in my class.
   a. one of the tallest b. the tallest   c. taller

4. Fatima and Dalia are sisters, but they don't look _____.
   a. same   b. like   c. alike

5. The new restaurant is not _____ the old one.
   a. so good   b. good as   c. as good as

6. John is short, but his daughter, Mary, _____.
   a. can't   b. doesn't   c. isn't

7. James is funny, but Lisa is _____ than he is.
   a. the most funny   b. funnier   c. funniest

8. Please drive _____. It's snowing outside.
   a. carefully   b. careful   c. as carefully

9. English is _____ Korean in several ways.
   a. different   b. different from   c. different than

10. Are these pictures similar or _____?
    a. different from   b. different   c. more different

B. Write a paragraph of five sentences and compare two people that you know well. Include age, personal appearance, talents, and abilities.

Example: _____ *Sara and Ricardo are two of my friends. Sara is older than Ricardo.*

_____

_____

_____

_____

_____

_____

_____

_____

_____

_____

_____

_____

_____

C. Correct the errors in comparison.

New York City and Seattle are cities in the United States. New York is most

crowded than Seattle. It has tallest buildings and more traffic. People in New York

City are in a hurry and walk fast than people in Seattle. Seattle is more quiet than

New York City. It is rainy than New York and warmer in the winter.

CHAPTER 10
Expressing Ideas with Verbs

■ **Quiz 1:** SHOULD and LET'S.

Write responses, using **should** or **let's**.

Example: **A:** I feel very dizzy.

B: _____You should see a doctor._____

1. **A:** We have 15 minutes before class starts.

   B: Let's _____.

2. **A:** I'm going to go to an important meeting early tomorrow morning.

   B: You should _____.

3. **A:** I can't fall asleep.

   B: You should _____.

4. **A:** I need to buy a new dress for the party.

   B: Let's _____.

5. **A:** It's snowing very hard outside.

   B: You shouldn't _____.

6. **A:** I'm thirsty.

   B: Let's _____.

7. **A:** The weather is beautiful outside today.

   B: Let's _____.

8. **A:** I need more money.

   B: You should _____.

9. **A:** My feet are hurting me.

   B: You should _____.

10. **A:** It's Alan's birthday today.

    B: Really! Let's _____.

■ Quiz 2: MUST and HAVE TO.

Using **must** and **have to**, give advice in response to each question.

Example: **A:** I would like to have healthy green plants. What do I have to do?

   B: *You must water your plants and give them some*

   sunlight every day.

1. I would like to be in your English class. What do I have to do?

_____

_____

2. I would like to learn to speak your language. What do I need to do?

_____

_____

3. I would like to become a doctor. What do I have to do?

_____

_____

4. I am interested in getting a driver's license. What do I have to do?

_____

_____

5. I would like to pass this course. What do I have to do?

_____

_____

■ **Quiz 3:** Review of modals.

Complete the sentences with *can, could, may, would, must, should,* or *have to.* **More** than one modal may fit a sentence, and the modal may be positive or negative.

Example: If Frank gets a new job, he _____*may*_____ move to another city.

1. _____ you like to meet me for dinner after class?

2. We _____ go out tonight if we find a babysitter.

3. You _____ smoke so much. It's bad for your health.

4. _____ you open a window, please? It's stuffy in here.

5. Clarence doesn't _____ call me later. I'll see him tomorrow.

6. The bill is past due. You _____ pay it immediately.

7. It _____ rain tonight. Take an umbrella.

8. Ricardo _____ play the guitar very well.

9. Lisa looked for you, but she _____ find you.

10. If you don't study, you _____ pass this course.

■ **Quiz 4:** Present and past progressive.

Write a question for each answer, based on the cues.

Example: **A:** _____*Were you studying at the library yesterday afternoon?*_____
     B: No, I wasn't. (I wasn't studying at the library yesterday afternoon.)

1. **A:** _____
   B: Yes, I am. (I am taking a quiz now.)

2. **A:** _____
   B: No, I wasn't. (I wasn't taking a test yesterday at 10:00 A.M.)

3. **A:** _____
   B: Yes, he is. (My teacher is standing in front of the class today.)

4. **A:** _____
   B: Yes, he was. (My teacher was standing in front of the class yesterday.)

5. **A:** _____
   B: Yes, they were. (My classmates were doing their homework last night.)

■ Quiz 5:   WHILE, WHEN, and simple past versus past progressive.

Complete the paragraphs with verbs in the SIMPLE PAST or the PAST PROGRESSIVE.

> | cook | sleep |

Example: Sara ___*was cooking*___ this morning while her children ___*were sleeping*___ .

> | eat | ring | pick | answer | finish | call |

1. While I _____ dinner yesterday evening, the phone

   _____ . I _____ it up, but no one

   _____ . When I _____ dinner, someone

   _____ again. It was a wrong number.

> | wait | meet | be | turn |

2. George _____ his wife, Rachel, when he _____

   20 years old. They _____ in line at the college cafeteria during

   lunch. George _____ around and noticed the beautiful red-haired

   girl behind him.

■ Quiz 6:   FOR and SINCE.

Complete the sentences with *for* or *since* and information about you. Each pair of sentences should have similar meanings.

Example: I have enjoyed sports since _____ *I was 6 years old.* _____ .

I have enjoyed sports for _____ *twenty years* _____ .

1. I have studied English since _____ .

   I have studied English for _____ .

2. I have been in this class since _____ .

   I have been in this class for _____ .

3. I have lived here since _____ .

   I have lived here for _____ .

4. I have worked since _____ .

   I have worked for _____ .

5. My parents have known each other since _____ .

   My parents have known each other for _____ .

■ **Quiz 7:** Present perfect questions and NEVER/EVER.

A. Write a question for each answer.

Example: **A:** _____*Have you ever been to Amsterdam?*_____
   B: Yes, I have. (I have been to Amsterdam.)

1. **A:** _____
   B: Yes, they have. (My parents have visited the United States.)

2. **A:** _____
   B: No, I haven't. (I've never been to an amusement park.)

3. **A:** _____
   B: Yes, he has. (Ben has worked for an international company.)

4. **A:** _____
   B: Yes, she has. (Kyoung Sun has read a book in English.)

5. **A:** _____
   B: No, they haven't. (Mr. and Mrs. Johnson have never been to Hawaii.)

B. Write answers for the questions. Use **never** if the answer is negative. Do not use short answers.

Example: **A:** Have you ever seen snow?
   B: _____*No, I've never seen snow.*_____

6. **A:** Have you ever skied?

   B: _____

7. **A:** Have you ever had a picnic on the beach at sunset?

   B: _____

8. **A:** Have you ever been to a baseball game?

   B: _____

9. **A:** Have you ever met a famous person?

   B: _____

10. **A:** Have you ever baked bread?

   B: _____

■ **Quiz 8:** Irregular past participles and HOW LONG questions.

Correct the errors, if any.

Example: Mr. and Mrs. Jones ~~has~~ *have* been to San Francisco.

1. How long have you knew your husband?

2. That is the most beautiful sunset I ever seen.

3. I'm so happy you called. We didn't spoken for a very long time.

4. How long are you been here? I'm sorry I'm so late.

5. Hiroko have never gone to a dance club.

6. **A:** How long have you that car?

   B: For about two years.

7. **A:** How long have you worked in this restaurant?

   B: For about a year.

8. Mrs. Jackson is very conservative. She never worn a pair of slacks.

9. Please do not throw out the newspaper. I haven't red it.

10. Mrs. Smith has meet the president of the United States.

■ CHAPTER 10 TEST

A. Choose the best answer.

1. I had a very bad earache yesterday morning. I _____ to the doctor last night.
   a. should go   b. must go   c. had to go

2. According to the law, a person _____ be an adult to buy alcohol.
   a. has   b. must   c. can

3. Fumiko _____ to play the guitar very well.
   a. can to   b. is able   c. can

4. While _____ television last night, the lights in my apartment went off.
   a. I watched   b. I have watched   c. I was watching

5. Mr. Rice has been a doctor _____ .
   a. since 1980   b. since 20 years   c. 20 years ago

6. Have you _____ to France?
   a. went   b. ever go   c. ever been

7. My teacher _____ me at home yesterday.
   a. called   b. has called   c. was calling

8. How long _____ that car?
   a. Tom has   b. has Tom   c. has Tom had

9. I'm hungry. _____ go get lunch.
   a. Let's   b. Should   c. We

10. My parents _____ me yesterday when you called.
    a. visited   b. were visiting   c. are visiting

B. Write a question for each response.

1. **A:** _____
   B: Yes, I can. (I can speak Japanese fluently.)

2. **A:** _____
   B: Of course. (I can close the window.)

3. **A:** _____
   B: No, I haven't. (I have never been to Australia.)

4. **A:** _____
   B: About 10 years. (I've lived at my present address for about 10 years.)

5. **A:** _____
   B: I was washing the dishes. (I was washing the dishes when you called.)

6. **A:** _____
   B: You have to take an entrance exam. (You have to take an entrance exam
   before you can get into my school.)

7. **A:** _____
   B: Last week. (I bought that dress last week.)

8. **A:** _____
   B: No, I wasn't. (I wasn't able to attend class yesterday.)

9. **A:** _____
   B: He's taking an exam. (Mike is taking an exam now.)

10. **A:** _____
    B: No, he wasn't. (Mike wasn't taking an exam at 10:00 yesterday morning.)

C. Correct the verb errors.

While I was reading a book yesterday evening, I was hearing a knock at my door.

I open the door and was so happy to see my friends Lisa and Ricardo. They were

carry a cake and some balloons. They said, "Surprise! Happy birthday!" I was felt so

happy. I make some coffee and then we enjoyed the cake together.

Final Exam

A. Choose the best answer.

1. What time _____ last night?
   a. did you arrive   b. are you arriving   c. you arrived

2. Mary _____ with her friends tomorrow.
   a. goes to have lunch   c. will to have lunch
   b. is going to have lunch

3. Don't worry. Frank is going to be back _____.
   a. five minutes   b. five minutes ago   c. in five minutes

4. Sam went running _____.
   a. last week   b. last weeks   c. next week

5. **A:** When _____ home?
   B: At 10:00 P.M.
   a. will be you   b. you will be   c. will you be

6. What _____ when you wake up every morning?
   a. you doing   b. you will do   c. do you do

7. If _____, the school will close for the day.
   a. it will snow   b. it snows   c. it is going to snow

8. Before Albert _____ to bed tonight, he will telephone his parents in Germany.
   a. is going   b. will go   c. goes

9. Did you _____ to buy milk at the supermarket?
   a. forget   b. forgot   c. forgetting

10. **A:** Can Thomas play the drums?

    B: No, he _____.
    a. didn't   b. couldn't   c. can't

11. I don't _____ change a flat tire.
    a. know to   b. can't   c. know how to

12. It is _____ cold to go swimming.
    a. very   b. too   c. enough

13. You cooked _____ food for dinner. We will have to finish it tomorrow.
    a. enough   b. too many   c. too much

14. This room is not _____ for 100 people.
    a. big enough   b. big   c. enough big

15. Arthur went to buy some _____ milk.
    a. many   b. more   c. much

16. _____ meet me for coffee on Thursday afternoon?
    a. Can you   b. May you   c. Can

17. _____ you close the door, please?
    a. Could   b. May   c. Do

18. _____ sit in that chair. It's broken.
    a. Not to   b. No   c. Don't

19. My favorite team _____ the football game yesterday.
    a. wins   b. won   c. was win

20. I didn't sleep well last night. I _____ sleepy all morning.
    a. have felt   b. was felt   c. feel

21. Peggy bought _____ at the jewelry store.
    a. a gold expensive necklace   c. an expensive gold necklace
    b. a gold and expensive necklace

22. _____ the people in this class speak more than one language.
    a. Almost   b. Most   c. Almost all of

23. _____ teenagers like to listen to music.
    a. Most   b. Most of   c. All of

24. My _____ apartment is very small.
    a. friend's   b. friend   c. friend is

25. That's not your pen, it's _____.
    a. my   b. I   c. mine

26. Mr. and Mrs. Rice own that boat. It's _____.
    a. theirs   b. they're   c. there's

27. _____ coat is that?
    a. Who is   b. Who's   c. Whose

28. Give _____.
    a. Susan's ball   b. Susan the ball   c. the ball for Susan

29. Mrs. Jackson _____.
    a. told a bedtime story her children   c. told her children a bedtime story
    b. told to her children a bedtime story

30. Can you fix the radio _____?
    a. to me   b. for me   c. mine

31. Japanese is _____ English.
    a. different from   b. different   c. different than

32. Do your children look _____?
    a. like   b. alike   c. same

33. Limes are _____ lemons in some ways.
    a. same as   b. like   c. similar

34. John's car is _____ than mine.
    a. more cheap   b. expensive   c. less expensive

35. My brother is _____ than I am.
    a. younger   b. more young   c. youngest

36. Carlos is wealthy, but Gina _____.
    a. doesn't   b. hasn't   c. isn't

37. Rita is the _____ of all my friends.
    a. smartest   b. smarter   c. smart

38. Mr. Wilson is _____ chess players in our town.
    a. one of the best   b. better   c. the best

39. Please write _____. It is difficult to read your handwriting.
    a. neat   b. neater   c. neatly

40. **A:** I feel terrible. I have a bad stomachache.

    B: You _____ see a doctor.
    a. may   b. should   c. will

41. Do we _____ go home now? I am enjoying myself.
    a. have to   b. must   c. need

42. You _____ work hard if you want to succeed.
    a. can   b. might   c. must

43. Mr. Jackson _____ to lift 200 pounds easily when he was a young man.
    a. should   b. may   c. was able

44. While I was watching television, my father _____.
    a. was calling   b. is calling   c. called

45. Sam has known Mary _____ he was a child.
    a. when   b. for   c. since

46. Have you _____ been to New Orleans?
    a. not   b. ever   c. was

47. How _____ have you been in this country?
    a. much   b. many   c. long

48. When class started, we _____ our textbooks.
    a. are taking out   b. have taken out   c. took out

49. _____ John at home last night when you went to visit?
    a. Has been   b. Was   c. Were

50. Michael has lived in that house _____.
    a. for twenty years   b. twenty years ago   c. in twenty years

B. Write ten sentences about what you did last week and what you are planning to do this week and on the weekend.

_____

_____

_____

_____

_____

_____

_____

_____

_____

_____

_____

_____

Answer Key

CHAPTER 1

■ Quiz 1

1. is a language, is a country
2. are countries, are languages
3. is a city, are cities
4. are insects, is an insect
5. is a month, are months
6. are seasons, is a season
7. is a continent, are continents
8. is a flower, are flowers
9. are machines, is a machine
10. is a bird, are birds

■ Quiz 2

1. isn't . . . is young
   isn't . . . is happy
   isn't . . . is fast
2. isn't . . . is square
   aren't . . . are beautiful
   aren't . . . are open
   aren't . . . are soft
3. isn't . . . is new
   isn't . . . is expensive
   isn't . . . is angry

■ Quiz 3

1. in	4. behind	7. in
2. at	5. on	8. on
3. on	6. next to	9. above

■ Quiz 4

1. **d**	6. c
2. j	7. e
3. a	8. g
4. f	9. i
5. b	10. h

■ Quiz 5

To the teacher: Correct sentences that use vocabulary and the verbs *be* and *have* are acceptable.

■ Quiz 6

To the teacher: Students are likely to confuse the sounds of *this* and *these* as well as the use of the apostrophe.

■ Quiz 7

1. What is a cat?
2. Who are those people?
3. Who is that?
4. What is your favorite class?
5. What are their names? (*or* a variation such as "What are your friends' names?")
6. What is his name? (*or* a variation such as "What is your friend's name?")
7. What is her telephone number?
8. Who is her teacher?
9. What is a camel?
10. What is a Cadillac?

■ CHAPTER 1 TEST

A. To the teacher: Correct sentences using the present tense accurately with proper subject-verb agreement are acceptable.
Example for Yoko: Yoko comes from Tokyo, Japan. She is married. She has black hair and brown eyes. She is 25 years old.

B.
1. Is Marta your wife?
2. Are these your classmates?
3. Is Sonia tall?
4. Are you at home right now?
5. Is Sam tired?

6. What are Montreal and Miami?

7. What's her name?

8. Is Kate married?

9. What is this?

10. Who is your favorite teacher?

C. 1. on, on, in, between, next to, beside

D. 1. on, next to, under, behind

CHAPTER 2

■ Quiz 1

1. always wakes up

2. usually gets up

3. always read

4. always leaves

5. never drives

6. always drives

7. seldom eat

8. is never

9. usually writes

10. often thinks

■ Quiz 2

1. Pablo and Ali do <u>their</u> homework together every evening.

2. I go to work at 8:00 A.M. My husband <u>goes</u> at 9:00 A.M.

3. We often go to museums with <u>our</u> friends.

4. Anna <u>has</u> lunch with her mother on Tuesday afternoons.

5. John and <u>his</u> wife always have breakfast together.

6. Carol and Paul <u>go</u> downtown every day.

7. Tom always <u>has</u> a snack at 10 P.M.

8. Mr. and Mrs. Rice <u>have</u> two sons.

9. Anita has a new dress. <u>Her</u> dress is red and white.

10. I <u>do</u> my work.

■ Quiz 3

1. **A:** Does ____ have curly hair?
   B: Yes, he/she does. *or* No, he/she doesn't.

2. **A:** Is ____ in class today?
   B: Yes, he/she is. *or* No, he/she isn't.

3. **A:** Does ____ speak English fluently?
   B: Yes, he/she does. *or* No, he/she doesn't.

4. **A:** Does ____ have a good sense of humor?
   B: Yes, he/she does. *or* No, he/she doesn't.

5. **A:** Does ____ live near the school?
   B: Yes, he/she does. *or* No, he/she doesn't.

■ Quiz 4

1. Where are you from?

2. Where do you work?

3. When do your morning classes begin?

4. When do you usually have lunch?

5. When does the movie start?

■ Quiz 5

To the teacher: Students may confuse *have* and *has*, *do* and *does*, and *go* and *goes*.

■ Quiz 6

1. It is 7:00 P.M. in Chicago now.

2. It is 6:00 P.M. in Denver now.

3. It is 5:00 P.M. in Los Angeles now.

4. It is 4:00 P.M. in Anchorage now.

5. It is 3:00 P.M. in Honolulu now.

■ Quiz 7

1. It is warm and rainy in Seattle today.

2. It is hot and sunny in Los Angeles today.

3. It is cool and cloudy in Chicago today.

4. It is warm and sunny in New York today.

5. It is hot and rainy in Miami today.

■ CHAPTER 2 TEST

A.
1. Where does Samir live?
2. Do you like ice cream?
3. What is the date today?
4. What is the weather today?
5. Is Chicago usually cold in the winter?
6. Are you a doctor?
7. What time/When do you usually eat lunch?
8. What time/When does the movie begin?
9. What time/When does the plane arrive?
10. Who is that man?

B. To the teacher: Correct sentences using proper placement of adverbs and agreement of subject and verb are acceptable.

C.
1. It is 6:00 P.M.
2. Anita works at home.
3. Ken meets me every Sunday for dinner and a movie.
4. We usually have lunch from 12:00 P.M to 1:00 P.M.
5. The department stores open on Mondays at 10:00 A.M.
6. My pants are under my bed.
7. The glasses are on to the table.
8. It is cloudy today.
9. It isn't warm in Chicago in the winter.
10. We don't see you in class anymore.

CHAPTER 3

■ Quiz 1

To the teacher: Make sure that the personal pronoun is clear in each case.

■ Quiz 2

1. Where is the man sitting?
2. Why is the man calling the waiter?
3. Where is the waiter going?
4. Why is the man happy?
5. What is the man eating?

■ Quiz 3

1. B. is reading
2. A. call
3. C. are calling
4. B. have
5. C. is cooking
6. A. plays
7. C. wins, is winning
8. B. is taking
9. B. is writing
10. A. walks

■ Quiz 4

1. cooks, is cooking, are waiting, smells
2. **A:** hear
   A: know . . . think
   B: He's (*or* He is) singing
3. **A:** Did . . . see
   B: are . . . looking
   A: is sitting . . . is
   B: is . . . see

■ Quiz 5

To the teacher: All correctly structured sentences with logical endings are acceptable.

■ Quiz 6

1. **A:** Is
   B: Yes, there is.
2. **A:** Are
   B: Yes, there are.
3. **A:** Is
   B: Yes, there is.
4. **A:** Are
   B: No, there aren't.
5. **A:** Is
   B: No, there isn't.

1. are . . . around
2. are . . . between
3. is next to (*or* near)
4. are . . . around
5. are . . . inside
6. is, far away from
7. is next to
8. is on
9. is far away from
10. is in the middle of / between / near

■ CHAPTER 3 TEST

A. 1. C. are reading
2. B. are clapping
3. C. speak
4. C. am thinking
5. B. is raining
6. C. is he wearing
7. B. hear
8. C. doesn't want
9. C. meet
10. C. am writing

B. 1. Would you like some coffee?
2. Do you think that English grammar is difficult?
3. Do you need a new car?
4. Are there many students in this school?
5. Does it rain often in the winter in the United States?
6. Do you smell smoke?
7. Do bananas taste sweet?
8. Are you taking an exam?
9. Where are you going?
10. Are you happy?

C. 1. in back of
2. in the front of
3. in the middle of

4. in the back of
5. next to
6. in back of
7. next to (*or* in front of)
8. in front of
9. in the middle of
10. in front of

CHAPTER 4

■ Quiz 1

1. young-**ADJ**
man-**S**/**NOUN**
new-**ADJ**
suit-**OV**

2. Carla-**S**/**NOUN**
interesting-**ADJ**
movie-**OV**
television-**OP**

3. You-**S**/**NOUN**
dark-**ADJ**
colors-**OV**
I-**S**/**NOUN**
light-**ADJ**
colors-**OV**

4. Mr. and Mrs. Smith-**S**/**NOUN**
fresh-**ADJ**
fish-**OV**
dinner-**OP**
Tuesdays-**OP**

5. Michael-**S**/**NOUN**
old-**ADJ**
car-**OV**
office-**OP**

6. Tom-**S**/**NOUN**
brown-**ADJ**
dog-**OV**

7. Yoko-**S**/**NOUN**
long-**ADJ**
letter-**OV**
parents-**OP**

8. Young-**ADJ**
girls-**S**/**NOUN**
dolls-**OP**

9. expensive-**ADJ**
   pen-**S**/**NOUN**
   Martha-**OP**

10. I-**S**/**NOUN**
    new-**ADJ**
    address-**OV**

■ Quiz 2

1. **A:** her
   B: He

2. it

3. It . . . They . . . them

4. **A:** him
   B: him

5. us . . . them

■ Quiz 3

To the teacher: Any nouns correctly written in the plural form and fitting each category are acceptable.

■ Quiz 4

To the teacher: Students should describe all the people in the picture.

■ Quiz 5

1. Most <u>countries</u> would like to have peace.

2. We get <u>homework</u> every day in this class.

3. How <u>many</u> tomatoes do you need?

4. Hiriko needs some <u>advice</u> about her schedule.

5. No change

6. He eats a lot of <u>vegetables</u>.

7. There is a lot of <u>traffic</u> in the city today.

8. The secretary has <u>information</u> about our company.

9. No change

10. No change

■ Quiz 6

To the teacher: Make sure the units of measure are correct in this exercise

■ Quiz 7

1. The
2. Ø
3. Ø
4. The
5. The
6. Ø
7. Ø
8. Ø . . . the
9. Ø
10. Ø

■ Quiz 8

1. b. something
2. c. anyone
3. b. someone
4. a. anyone
5. c. anything

■ CHAPTER 4 TEST

A.
1. b. milk
2. b. He
3. a. anything
4. c. them
5. c. you
6. c. No one
7. b. Love
8. c. music
9. b. us
10. a. It

B.
1. Knives
2. Oranges
3. traffic
4. potatoes
5. furniture
6. classes
7. women
8. cities
9. homework
10. information

C.
1. tall-**ADJ**
   man-**S**/**NOUN**
   beach-**OP**
   He-**S**/**NOUN**
   famous-**ADJ**
   photographer-**OV**
   He-**S**/**NOUN**
   pictures-**OV**
   people-**OP**
   water-**OP**
   people-**S**/**NOUN**
   him-**OP**

2. Clara-**s**/**NOUN**
animals-**OV**
She-**s**/**NOUN**
black-**ADJ**
cats-**OV**
large-**ADJ**
dog-**OV**
bright-**ADJ**
yellow-**ADJ**
birds-**OV**
house-**OP**
She-**s**/**NOUN**
them-**OP**
school-**OP**

3. Yoko-**s**/**NOUN**
surprise-**ADJ**
party-**OV**
birthday-**OP**
Yoko-**s**/**NOUN**
delicious-**ADJ**
cake-**OV**
She-**s**/**NOUN**
people-**OV**
party-**OP**

CHAPTER 5

■ Quiz 1

1. Were you at the gym on Thursday?

2. Were you at home yesterday?

3. Was your trip interesting?

4. Where were you last night?

5. Was Carlos at the concert last night?

■ Quiz 2

To the teacher: Correct original sentences that use the verbs and past time words in ways that make sense are acceptable.

■ Quiz 3

got . . . put . . . ate . . . left . . . rode . . . saw . . . drank . . . read . . . thought

■ Quiz 4

1. **A:** Did you see Helen yesterday morning?
   B: No, I didn't.

2. **A:** Did you sleep on the plane?
   B: Yes, I did.

3. **A:** Did you go to the library?
   B: No, I didn't.

4. **A:** Did Marco write this composition?
   B: No, he didn't.

5. **A:** Did you eat lunch at Sam's house?
   B: Yes, we did.

■ Quiz 5

1. **c**

2. d

3. e

4. b

5. a

■ Quiz 6

To the teacher: Correct original sentences that match the cues are acceptable.

■ Quiz 7

1. After I ate lunch, I took a walk. **or** I took a walk after I ate lunch.

2. When Jane met her husband, she was twenty years old. **or** Jane met her husband when she was twenty years old.

3. I didn't speak English before I came to this country. **or** Before I came to this country, I didn't speak English.

4. After he saw the fire, he called the fire department. **or** He called the fire department after he saw the fire.

5. When her parents left, the child started to cry.

■ CHAPTER 5 TEST

A.   1. Were you at the party last night?

2. Did you do the homework assignment?

3. Where did you go last night?

4. Why didn't you call me yesterday?

5. Who took you out to dinner yesterday?

6. Did you take the exam?

7. When did you have breakfast?

8. What does "ill" mean?

9. Was the play interesting?

10. Did it snow yesterday evening?

B. To the teacher: Original sentences that include the correct past form of the verb and time clauses are acceptable.

C.
1. Tony <u>went</u> to Ali's house last night.

2. Mariko called Tina <u>last</u> night about the homework assignment.

3. Where <u>were you</u> yesterday afternoon?

4. I <u>read</u> an interesting book when I was on vacation.

5. Tim <u>came</u> to this country after he finished high school.

6. Kim <u>watched</u> a funny television show last week.

7. Did Frank <u>meet</u> Pablo at the airport yesterday?

8. No change

9. I <u>drank</u> a cup of coffee before work.

10. No change

MIDTERM EXAM

A.
1. a. are animals
2. c. isn't
3. c. at home
4. c. your
5. b. Her
6. a. It's
7. b. My
8. c. has
9. c. Sam always comes
10. c. eat
11. b. is never late
12. c. do
13. c. goes
14. b. doesn't
15. c. What time do

16. c. It's
17. b. I'm wearing
18. c. are they
19. c. No, she isn't.
20. c. don't take
21. a. Did you understand
22. c. listening to
23. b. Would you like
24. b. thinks that
25. c. many students are there
26. c. it
27. c. children
28. b. some information
29. a. an
30. b. This
31. c. anything
32. b. them
33. c. cooked
34. b. stopped
35. b. wrote
36. c. two weeks ago
37. a. last night
38. c. in
39. c. at
40. c. on

B.
41. c. above
42. a. in
43. b. next to
44. c. under
45. c. between
46. b. in the middle of
47. a. in back of
48. a. in front of
49. b. far away from
50. c. outside

C. To the teacher: Correct sentences of description are acceptable.

CHAPTER 6

■ Quiz 1

1. is going to meet
   is going to dictate letters to
   is going to have
   is going to work
   is going to play

2. is going to teach
   is going to meet
   is going to see
   is going to go
   is going to prepare

■ Quiz 2

To the teacher: Original sentences that use the past and future tense verbs correctly and time words that make sense are acceptable.

■ Quiz 3

1. will get married . . . will say . . . will leave
2. will wash . . . will drive

■ Quiz 4

To the teacher: Original questions that use the future time correctly are acceptable.

■ Quiz 5

1. may/might
1. Maybe
3. Maybe
4. may/might
5. may/might
6. may/might
7. Maybe
8. Maybe
9. may/might
10. Maybe

■ Quiz 6

To the teacher: Original sentences that use future time clauses with **before**, **after**, and **when** are acceptable.

■ Quiz 7

To the teacher: Original sentences that use the conditional form correctly are acceptable.

■ CHAPTER 6 TEST

A.
1. c. is
2. c. yesterday
3. c. in a few minutes
4. a. in two more weeks
5. b. may
6. b. are you
7. c. she comes
8. a. Before
9. a. Are they
10. b. Will you be

B. To the teacher: Original sentences that use the future time and **before**, **after**, **when**, and *if-* clauses correctly are acceptable.

C.
1. What <u>do you</u> do on Friday evenings?
2. Right now, we <u>are</u> <u>writing</u> an exam.
3. I <u>may</u>/<u>might</u> play tennis with Susan tomorrow evening.
4. **A:** No change
   B: No, he <u>won't</u>.
5. Jake is <u>going</u> to the gym now.
6. I <u>am</u> going to meet you before class tomorrow.
7. **A:** No change
   B: I <u>may</u> <u>be</u>.
8. We won't ~~to~~ see each other tomorrow.
9. <u>Are</u> Max and James going to work together on the report?
10. We will meet <u>in</u> one week ~~ago~~.

Chapter 7

■ Quiz 1

1. **A:** know how to
   A: Can
   B: can't . . . can't / couldn't

2. **A:** couldn't
   B: Can

3. **A:** know how to

4. **A:** Can
   B: can't

5. **A:** Can

■ Quiz 2

1. This dress is too ~~much~~ small, so I can't wear it.

2. Ricardo <u>can't</u> afford the car because it's too expensive.

3. Joe has too ~~many~~ <u>much</u> work to do. He can't speak with you now.

4. The size of our class is perfect. There aren't too ~~much~~ <u>many</u> people.

5. I feel ~~too~~ <u>very</u> tired. I'd like to go to sleep now.

■ Quiz 3

1. too hot

2. too expensive . . . enough money

3. too young . . . old enough

4. enough time . . . too busy

5. too heavy . . . strong enough

6. too full

■ Quiz 4

A. To the teacher: Correct original sentences that are variations of the answers below are acceptable.

1. Can I borrow your dictionary?

2. Could you open the window, please?

3. Excuse me, can you tell me what yesterday's homework was?

4. Would you like a cup of coffee?

5. Could you turn down the music, please?

B. To the teacher: Correct original sentences are acceptable.

■ Quiz 5

A. 1. d
2. e
3. a
4. b
5. c

B. 1. Be careful.
2. Please close the window. (*or* another polite variation)
3. Walk two blocks to 14th Street.
4. Stop! Thief!

■ Quiz 6

1. **A:** at
   B: in

2. in

3. at

4. in

5. in

6. in . . . at

7. in . . . in

■ Chapter 7 Test

A. 1. b. know how to
2. a. weren't able
3. b. too heavy
4. c. Would you
5. c. could
6. c. warm enough
7. a. please sit down
8. c. know how to
9. c. too many
10. c. too tired

1. What would you like to order?

2. Would you like some coffee?

3. Can I speak with you?

4. Excuse me, where can I find the carrots?

5. Can I borrow your pen?

C.
1. in
2. at
3. at
4. in
5. in

CHAPTER 8

■ Quiz 1

1. favorite Italian restaurant

2. dark blue suit

3. big white house

4. antique glass vases

5. intelligent young people

6. large, colorful paintings

7. small, black address book

8. tall, handsome man

9. sweet ripe peaches

10. serious young woman

■ Quiz 2

■ Quiz 3

1. Whose bag is that? It's <u>Rita's</u>.

2. That coat is mine. It's not <u>yours</u>.

3. <u>Hiroko's</u> husband works for a large computer company.

4. Mark and Susan live in Colorado. <u>Their</u> house is in the Rocky Mountains.

5. Peggy isn't at home now, but ~~shes~~ <u>her</u> sister is.

6. <u>Our</u> class has many nice people.

7. Please give ~~she~~ <u>her</u> the message.

8. That's my cousin. ~~He's~~ <u>His</u> name is Sam.

9. ~~His~~ He's studying at our college.

10. I bought a new suit and paid for ~~its~~ <u>it</u> by check.

■ Quiz 4

■ Quiz 5

1. My friends sent me a postcard from Korea.

2. Can you lend me your dictionary?

3. Frank showed us his new car.

4. Minako gave her dog a bath.

5. Sam opened the door for his wife.

6. The mechanic fixed my car for me.

7. The teacher answered a question for me.

8. John wrote a letter to his parents.

9. Maria handed the book to me.

10. My wife cashed a check for me.

■ Quiz 6

■ CHAPTER 8 TEST

A.
1. a. a young Italian

2. c. dark blue wool

3. c. Most

4. b. One of

5. a. him

6. c. me

7. b. John's

8. a. Whose

9. c. for his wife

10. c. introduced her father to me

B. To the teacher: Correct sentences that use adjectives, nouns, and noun modifiers are acceptable.

C. George and Maria came to this country in May. ~~Their~~ They came from Brazil. All of ~~they~~ their family lives in Brazil. He is an intelligent young engineer. ~~His~~ He's studying English in a language school.

Maria is a children's dentist. ~~Her~~ She is studying English reading, writing, and conversation with a private tutor. ~~She's~~ Her private tutor is American.

CHAPTER 9

■ Quiz 1

1. John's haircut is <u>the</u> same as mine.
2. Hiroko and Minako are twins. They look ~~like~~ <u>alike</u>.
3. British English is different ~~than~~ <u>from</u> American English in certain ways.
4. Are my homework answers similar ~~with~~ <u>to</u> yours?
5. A motorcycle is ~~alike~~ <u>like</u> a bicycle in some ways.
6. We signed up for this class at <u>the</u> same time.
7. Jack's handwriting is similar <u>to</u> his brother's.
8. English and Spanish are similar ~~to~~ in some ways, but different in other ways.
9. Love is ~~alike~~ <u>like</u> a rose.
10. Marie and Jean come from <u>the</u> same country.

■ Quiz 2

1. smaller . . . faster . . . heavier . . . longer
2. older . . . more educated . . . more famous . . . funnier . . . more serious . . . more conservative

■ Quiz 3

To the teacher: Different answers are acceptable for some of the items.

1. Silver isn't as expensive as gold. Silver is less expensive than gold.
2. Water isn't as sweet as grape juice.
3. Money is less important than health. Money isn't as important as health.
4. Walking isn't as exciting as skydiving. Walking is less exciting than skydiving.
5. A cloud is less colorful than a rainbow. A cloud isn't as colorful as a rainbow.

■ Quiz 4

1. e
2. a
3. d
4. b
5. c

■ Quiz 5

To the teacher: Correct sentences using the forms below are acceptable.

1. one of the best actors in the movies
2. one of the most important people in this country
3. one of the most expensive cars
4. one of the most interesting people that I know
5. one of the best places to take a vacation

■ Quiz 6

1. hard-**ADV**
2. easy-**ADJ**
3. carefully-**ADV**
4. well-**ADV**
5. quickly-**ADV** . . . slowly-**ADV**
6. early-**ADJ**
7. late-**ADV**
8. good-**ADJ**
9. perfectly-**ADV**
10. fast-**ADJ**

1. more beautifully than
2. as hard as
3. more fluently than
4. as well as
5. as quickly as
6. as often as
7. as early as
8. as neatly as
9. as fast as
10. more carefully than

■ CHAPTER 9 TEST

A.
1. c. one of the most intelligent
2. c. larger than
3. b. the tallest
4. c. alike
5. c. as good as
6. c. isn't
7. b. funnier
8. a. carefully
9. b. different from
10. b. different

B. **To the teacher:** Correct sentences using comparisons are acceptable.

C. New York City and Seattle are cities in the United States. New York is <u>more</u> crowded than Seattle. It has <u>taller</u> buildings and more traffic. People in New York City are in a hurry and walk <u>faster</u> than people in Seattle. Seattle is ~~more~~ <u>quieter</u> than New York City. It is <u>rainier</u> than New York and warmer in the winter.

CHAPTER 10

■ Quiz 1

To the teacher: Variations of the sentences below are acceptable.

1. take a walk. / get a coke, etc.
2. go to sleep early
3. drink some hot milk
4. go shopping
5. drive now
6. get a drink
7. go to the park
8. get another job
9. buy better shoes
10. have a party!

■ Quiz 2

To the teacher: Correct sentences using **must** or **have to** are acceptable.

Example: You have to go to the Registrar's Office.

■ Quiz 3

1. Would
2. may / might
3. shouldn't
4. Could / Would / Can
5. have to
6. must / should
7. may / might
8. can
9. couldn't
10. may not / won't

■ Quiz 4

1. Are you taking a quiz now?
2. Were you taking a test yesterday at 10:00 A.M.?
3. Is your teacher standing in front of the class today?
4. Was your teacher standing in front of the class yesterday?
5. Were your classmates doing their homework last night?

1. was eating . . . rang . . . picked . . . answered . . . finished . . . called

2. met . . . was . . . were waiting . . . turned

■ Quiz 6

To the teacher: Correct sentences using *for* and *since* are acceptable.

■ Quiz 7

A. 1. Have your parents visited the United States?

2. Have you ever been to an amusement park?

3. Has Ben worked for an international company?

4. Has Kyoung Sun read a book in English?

5. Have Mr. and Mrs. Johnson ever been to Hawaii?

B. 1. No, I've never skied. *or* Yes, I've skied.

2. No, I've never had a picnic on the beach at sunset. *or* Yes, I've had a picnic on the beach at sunset.

3. No, I've never been to a baseball game. *or* Yes, I've been to a baseball game.

4. No, I've never met a famous person. *or* Yes, I've met a famous person.

5. No, I've never baked bread. *or* Yes, I've baked bread.

■ Quiz 8

1. How long have you ~~knew~~ known your husband?

1. That is the most beautiful sunset I've ever seen.

3. I'm so happy you called. We ~~didn't~~ haven't spoken for a very long time.

4. How long ~~are~~ have you been here? I'm sorry I'm so late.

5. Hiroko ~~have~~ has never gone to a dance club.

6. **A:** How long have you had that car?
    B: For about two years.

7. No change

8. Mrs. Jackson is very conservative. She has never worn a pair of slacks.

9. Please do not throw out the newspaper. I haven't ~~red~~ read it.

10. Mrs. Smith has ~~meet~~ met the president of the United States.

■ **CHAPTER 10 TEST**

A. 1. c. had to go

1. b. must

3. b. is able

4. c. I was watching

5. a. since 1980

6. c. ever been

7. a. called

8. c. has Tom had

9. a. Let's

10. b. were visiting

B. 1. Can you speak Japanese fluently?

2. Can you close the window?

3. Have you ever been to Australia?

4. How long have you lived at your present address?

5. What were you doing when I called?

6. What do you have to do before you can get into your school?

7. When did you buy that dress?

8. Were you able to attend class yesterday?

9. What's Mike doing now?

10. Was Mike taking an exam at 10:00 yesterday morning?

C.   While I was reading a book yesterday evening, I ~~was hearing~~ <u>heard</u> a knock at my door. I ~~open~~ <u>opened</u> the door and was so happy to see my friends Lisa and Ricardo. They were ~~carry~~ <u>carrying</u> a cake and some balloons. They said, "Surprise! Happy birthday!" I ~~was~~ felt so happy. I ~~make~~ <u>made</u> some coffee, and then we enjoyed the cake together.

FINAL EXAM

A.
1. a. did you arrive
2. b. is going to have lunch
3. c. in five minutes
4. a. last week
5. c. will you be
6. c. do you do
7. b. it snows
8. c. goes
9. a. forget
10. c. can't
11. c. know how to
12. b. too
13. c. too much
14. a. big enough
15. b. more
16. a. Can you
17. a. Could
18. c. Don't
19. b. won
20. a. have felt
21. c. an expensive gold necklace
22. c. Almost all of
23. a. Most
24. a. friend's
25. c. mine
26. a. theirs
27. c. Whose

28. b. Susan the ball
29. c. told her children a bedtime story
30. b. for me
31. a. different from
32. b. alike
33. b. like
34. c. less expensive
35. a. younger
36. c. isn't
37. a. smartest
38. a. one of the best
39. c. neatly
40. b. should
41. a. have to
42. c. must
43. c. was able
44. c. called
45. c. since
46. b. ever
47. c. long
48. c. took out
49. b. Was
50. a. for twenty years

B. To the teacher: Correct sentences that utilize past and future time are acceptable.